Paying for Crime

PAYING FOR CRIME
The Policies and Possibilities
of Crime Victim Reimbursement

SUSAN KISS SARNOFF

PRAEGER

Westport, Connecticut
London

Library of Congress Cataloging-in-Publication Data

Sarnoff, Susan Kiss.
    Paying for crime : the policies and possibilities of crime victim
reimbursement / Susan Kiss Sarnoff.
      p. cm.
    Includes bibliographical references and index.
    ISBN 0–275–95709–8 (alk. paper)
    1. Reparation—United States. 2. Victims of crimes—United
States. 3. Victims of crimes—Legal status, laws, etc.—United
States. I. Title.
HV8688.S25 1996
364.6′8—dc20   96–20683

British Library Cataloguing in Publication Data is available.

Library of Congress Catalog Card Number: 96–20683
ISBN: 0–275–95709–8

First published in 1996

Praeger Publishers, 88 Post Road West, Westport, CT 06881
An imprint of Greenwood Publishing Group, Inc.

Printed in the United States of America

The paper used in this book complies with the
Permanent Paper Standard issued by the National
Information Standards Organization (Z39.48–1984).

10 9 8 7 6 5 4 3 2 1

To Jerry

for his help,

to crime victims

for their needs,

and to the Mennonites

who care for one another

rather than relying on insurance

Contents

Illustrations

Preface

Thirty years ago Arthur Collins, traveling home on the New York City subway system, observed a deranged man harassing a woman in his subway car. Deflecting the man's attention from the woman saved her life but cost Arthur Collins his own.

Mr. Collins left a wife and young children virtually penniless. Occurring as it did when the Katherine ("Kitty") Genovese murder[1] was still a recent memory, Mr. Collins's murder and concern for his family prompted the New York state legislature to take two very important steps. First, it appropriated special funds for the Collins family. Then, so that no family would ever again have to face the economic fears that the Collins family had faced after Arthur Collins' murder, it created the New York State Crime Victims Compensation Board (today, the New York State Crime Victims' Board, to reflect that its role has expanded beyond compensating victims), to institutionalize compensation to innocent victims of violent crimes and their survivors. The New York board was the second state compensation program developed in the United States (California's was the first). The New York state program was much more comprehensive, however, and served as the model for the majority of subsequent state programs.

Today, three decades later, every state has established a victim compensation program. Their services have expanded to not only provide funds for victims and Good Samaritans, but to fund outreach programs to assist victims in obtaining compensation and other services. Rape crisis centers and battered women's shelters, which serve victims regardless of whether they report their crimes to the police, are also funded by state compensation programs. But opposition to these benefits continues, which is probably best reflected in these programs' low overall budgets.

As a result, many victims still have post victimization needs and costs, which go unmet even when they qualify for existing victim compensation. To what extent this is so, for how many victims, and whether it is the result of oversight, inadequate resources, intentionally or unintentionally exclusionary eligibility criteria, or other factors is unclear. The aim of this text is to identify the existing benefits available to victims of crime, as well as to explore their scopes and their limitations. It will also make recommendations for improvements to individual programs and to how they are coordinated with one another. Just as important, it has the aim of informing victims and those who assist them in meeting their needs of the availability of these benefits, so that lack of information need no longer be the sole reason that some victims have uncompensated needs.

ORGANIZATION OF THE TEXT

Chapter 1 begins with an overview of the needs of crime victims and the rationales and various forms of compensation provision. Chapters 2 through 6 are each devoted to a specific form of victim reimbursement. These chapters explore, respectively, restitution, private insurance, social welfare and other government benefit programs, civil litigation, and state crime victim compensation programs. Each of these chapters explores the state of the art of these benefits, their limitations, and options for their improvement. Chapters 7 and 8 will close the text by offering recommendations for cutting costs, enhancing revenues, expanding benefits, and otherwise improving the treatment of victims by improving how these services reach them and meet their needs; and by making broad recommendations to improve the provision of these benefits by coordinating, universalizing, and otherwise improving their delivery.

ACKNOWLEDGMENTS

No undertaking of this extent could be completed without the help, support, and resources of many mentors, colleagues, and friends. I have been generously blessed in this regard. First, I must thank my husband, Jerome Sarnoff, for his many readings, reviews, corrections and explanations of compensation law. I thank my children, Kristina Stevens and Stephen Mott, for their tolerance, and for the many times they cooked their own meals, and sometimes mine. I thank my mother, Theresa Kiss, for her financial as well as emotional encouragement and support, and my late father, Stephen Kiss, for inspiring me to be a compulsive reader, and for always admonishing me to question what I read. I thank my best friend, Patricia Chave, for always being there, as the model victim advocate she is.

I want to thank my editors, G. Nick Street and Marcia Goldstein, my production editor, Norine Mudrick, and my copyeditor, Kathleen Taylor, without whose help this text would probably never have seen print. I want to thank everyone at the Adelphi University School of Social Work for helping me not only to understand entitlements but to care about their effects on people. I must also thank them for making me believe that I, too, could contribute knowledge to the field of social work. These people include Risha Levinson, Amelia Chu, Eleanor Kremen, Gertrude Goldberg, Louise Skolnick, Joseph Vigilante, Lenard Kates, W. Cody Wilson, Narayan Viswanathan, Ralph Dolgoff, the late Alex Rosen, and the late Malvina Gordon. And I want to thank all my students, who have consistently challenged me to clarify—and confront—complex areas of social policy.

I want to thank all the staff members of the crime victim compensation programs who generously shared their data and time with me. In particular, I want to thank the staff of the New York State Crime Victims Board for their support and help with my research. Special thanks must be extended to Chairman Gennaro Fischetti, former Board Member Diane McGrath-McKechnie, and to Jerry, once again. I must also thank the late Geraldine Jordan, whose understanding of victims' needs inspired my work. And I must thank the past and present members of the New York State Crime Victims Board Advisory Council, whose activities on behalf of victims helped me to recognize gaps in service needs.

I must also thank the many people who helped me with my research, especially the staff of the National Criminal Justice Reference Service, particularly Stephanie Greenhouse and Skip Sigmun; Dr. Bertram S. Brown; Dan Eddy, Executive Director of the National Association of Crime Victim Compensation Boards; Regina Sobieski, Assistant Director for Victim Services and Research at Mothers Against Drunk Driving (MADD); my insurance agent, Michael Capaldo; and the staffs of the Swirbul Library at Adelphi University, the Davis Library at the College of Insurance, and the Garden City Library.

Finally, let me extend my thanks to all of the "victimologists" who paved the way for me to write this text, particularly Andrew Karmen and Robert Elias, who personally helped me during the early stages of my work. They have inspired and guided me more than they can ever know.

NOTE

1. Kitty Genovese was murdered on a New York City street while dozens of neighbors observed, but failed to act. Researchers have since concluded that their non-action was due to each individual's determination that, since there were so many witnesses, "someone else" was better able to handle the situation than they were. However, the public at the time attributed it to urban apathy, and efforts to increase citizens' concern for public safety proliferated after the incident.

Abbreviations

AFDC	Aid to Families with Dependent Children
COBRA	Consolidated Omnibus Budget Reconciliation Act
DBL	Disability Benefits (state-mandated or employer-provided)
EA	Emergency Assistance
EITC	Earned Income Tax Credit
FS	Food Stamps
HEAP	Home Energy Assistance Program
HR	Home Relief
ITD	Income Tax Deductions
LEAA	Law Enforcement Assistance Administration
MD	Medicaid
ME	Medicare
OASI	Old Age and Survivors' Insurance
OVC	Office for Victims of Crime
RR	Railroad Retirement
SSI	Supplemental Social Insurance
UI	Unemployment Insurance
VAWA	Violence Against Women Act
VB	Veterans' Benefits
VOCA	Victims of Crime Act
WC	Workers' Compensation

1

Introduction

During the past two decades Americans have become increasingly concerned about crime. While crime has not increased considerably over that time, perceptions of crime have. This has been due to the fact that, as other causes of injury have decreased, crime has become responsible for a greater proportion of injuries than in the past. It also results from increased media focus on crime (the proportion of media depictions of crime quadrupled from 1991 to 1995) (*Media Monitor* 1996).

Most of the concern about crime, too, has focused on offenders. Should prison terms be expanded? Should juveniles who commit "adult" crimes be punished as adults? What constitutes insanity, and when does it excuse crime?

While victims' rights have recently been expanded, many of these rights, too, focus on offenders. Most victims' rights can be exercised only in the courtroom; but, since many criminals are never caught (fewer than 22 percent of crimes and 48 percent of violent crimes have resulted in arrests since 1983) and the majority of those who are caught plea bargain their cases (in 1994, 77 percent of the offenders caught and charged with violent crimes entered guilty pleas), these laws actually affect few victims of crime (Maguire and Pastore 1994).

Although victims clearly have a stake in the prosecution and punishment of offenders, victims' needs resulting from crime extend far beyond the determination of offenders' fates. Victims of crime may require medical attention; treatment for shock or other reactions to trauma; wage replacement for time lost from work and financial assistance to pay for child care, housekeeping, and other help necessitated by their injuries or their need to act as witnesses against their attackers. In fact, in the United States, violent crime is responsible for 3 percent of medical spending, 10-20 percent of mental health care spending, and wage losses that amount to 1 percent of earnings (Miller, Cohen, and Wiersema 1996).

When victims die, family members may require assistance to pay for funerals and to replace income that would have been provided by the victims if they had lived. If victims are injured in ways that prevent them from earning a living, or from doing so in the same way they had before their injuries, victims or other members of their families may have to be trained to perform new skills.

These needs have not gone unrecognized. In fact, the provision of victim reimbursement predated the development of the criminal justice system.

However, in its historic form, reimbursement was always dependent on offenders' ability to pay it and victims' ability to collect it. This type of reimbursement often required installment payments, and the money almost never reached victims in time to meet their bills. It also presupposed that offenders had been caught and found guilty and that collection mechanisms were effective.

Therefore, such restitution-type reimbursement is clearly inadequate to meet the needs of most of the victims who incur costs as a result of crimes against them. Recognizing this, the United States has encouraged individual states to develop programs to compensate victims whether or not their offenders have been caught or convicted. This encouragement, in the form of matching funds, has resulted in all states enacting crime victim compensation programs of some type, although their benefit levels and eligibility requirements differ considerably.

But these programs also have many limitations, some of which were purposely created to avoid overlap with preexisting social services (such as Medicare for seniors injured during crimes). Other limitations reflect ideological opposition to income redistribution in general, opposition to providing benefits under particular circumstances (such as when victims contribute to their injuries), and attempts to conserve scarce resources. Therefore, it is vital that victim service providers understand the alternative government benefits available to people, which are not based on victim status but for which some crime victims may be eligible—particularly if they are not eligible for crime victim compensation.

It is vital, too, that victims and those who assist them understand the circumstances that make victims eligible for each type of benefit. (For example, most government benefits are based on the residency of the recipient. Moreover, workers' compensation is based on the location of the recipient's workplace, and crime victim compensation and restitution are based on where the crime occurred.)

These benefits are not inconsiderable. The federal Victims of Crime Act (VOCA) provides approximately $46 million per year in federal matching funds to states that add an additional $68 million, for a total of $114 million in crime victim compensation payments annually (Office for Victims of Crime, undated). Together with other government benefits and services to victims, the total increases to $8 billion (Miller, Cohen, and Wiersema 1996) demonstrating the amount of government benefits available from sources *other* than crime victim-specific reimbursement programs. However, as Figure 1.1 demonstrates, the bulk of victim costs are paid by private insurance—dwarfing victim-specific benefits as only .3 percent of the total. It should be noted, too, that even some government benefits, including workers' compensation, actually consist of private insurance benefits that are mandated and regulated by government. As they more closely resemble public than private benefits, they will be addressed in Chapter 4.

Therefore, it is advisable that all people, as potential victims of crime, consider the risk of wage or health benefit loss before they experience victimiza-

Figure 1.1
Distribution of Victim Costs
(by payment sources)

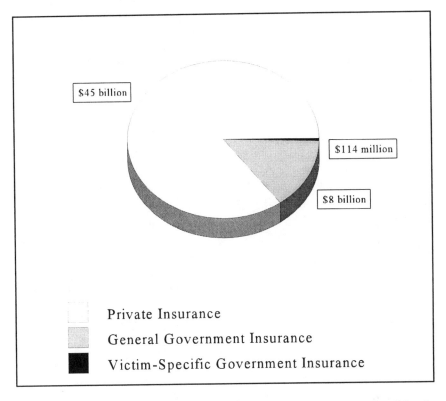

tion and insure themselves privately against them if they wish to maintain a lifestyle above that which government benefits permit. Victims and their advocates should, therefore, also be cognizant of private sector means of meeting victims' costs. As Figure 1.1 shows, private insurance pays $45 billion in victims' costs annually, or 85 percent of the total costs to victims, including most of the property loss that is reimbursed, because property loss is largely ignored by public benefit systems. Private insurance also covered pain and suffering, lost potential and other intangible benefits which can only be decided on individual bases, often requiring considerable litigation which also increase the outlays of private insurance. Finally, private insurance is also usually more generous and almost always more timely than public systems in the payments it makes to victims.

Even the most generous government benefits leave many indirect costs of victimization uncompensated. For example, neither crime victim compensation nor workers' compensation programs provide health benefits to the family members of victims who die or are unable to return to work as a result of crime, nor do they cover services for alcoholism or drug addiction precipitated by victimization.

Furthermore, no government benefits promise to maintain victims or their family members in the standard of living which they enjoyed prior to the crime; in fact, they provide no more than basic subsistence in most cases.

Finally, it should be understood that victims may initiate civil lawsuits against their assailants or anyone else (including corporate entities, and in limited cases, governmental ones) who can be held responsible for a crime's occurrence. Landlords, private security firms, schools, and businesses have been successfully sued for failing to take adequate precautions to protect people using their services, and payments in some such cases have been quite high. Again, however, not all crimes lend themselves to these types of lawsuits, and victims' needs have no relation to the potential for civil payments. Such cases also take years to litigate and take severe emotional tolls on victims (Barbieri 1989).

"Pain and suffering" payments are primarily awarded in the civil arena. This has the advantage that claims are determined individually, and far more liberally, than if awards were made statutorily uniform, as they would be if paid by a state compensation program (Spence 1989). However, very few victims receive awards for pain and suffering (Stark and Goldstein 1985).

Table 1.1 depicts the bulk of these benefits and identifies the types of needs reimbursed by each. From the table it is clear that government benefits differ widely in what they offer, but that private insurance and civil litigation generally cover more benefit categories than any government program.

This introduction will continue with an exploration of victims' needs caused by crime. It will then explore the rationales for reimbursing victims and the forms such reimbursement can take. Chapters 2 through 6 will explore in greater detail each of the means of reimbursing victims for their costs. Chapter 7 will explore ways that crime victim reimbursement and the criminal justice system can better serve victims, offer recommendations about how improvements to them could positively impact victims' receipt of reimbursement, and make recommendations for improving the provision of benefits and services to crime victims, whether victims are served by victim-specific or more generic agencies or service providers. Finally, Chapter 8 will explore how improving policy and service delivery and universalizing some benefits—particularly health benefits—could further simplify and improve services to victims, at less cost than is presently being expended.

VICTIMS' NEEDS CAUSED BY CRIME

The needs of crime victims are impacted by two sets of circumstances: the overall resources available to victims after crimes are committed and the level of need created by those crimes. For example, relatively minor crimes can cause considerable need for poor individuals with no health insurance or paid sick days, while wealthier individuals can be so seriously injured that their insurance and personal resources are inadequate to meet their expenses. Other factors to be considered when determining the level of need caused by crime are whether income maintenance programs and insurance policies cover the costs victims must

Table 1.1
Common Benefits and the Services They Cover [a]

BENEFIT	MEDICAL	MENTAL HEALTH	FUNERAL	WAGES/SUPPORT	ATTORNEY FEES	PROPERTY	PAIN & SUFFERING
AFDC [b]				A			
DISABILITY				A			
HILL-BURTON	S						
SSI [b]				A			
UNEMPLOYMENT [b]				A			
HOME RELIEF				A			
MEDICAID	A	A					
MEDICARE	A	A					
RR [b]				A			
OASI [b]				A			
VETERANS'				S			
VICTIM COMPENSATION	A	A	A	A	S	S	S
WORKERS' COMPENSATION	A	A	A	A	A		
RESTITUTION	A	A	A	A	S	A	S
PRIVATE INSURANCE	A	A	A	A		A	A
CIVIL LITIGATION	A	A	A	A	A	A	A

Notes:
[a] Data obtained from Goldberg (1991), see Bibliography.
[b] Can be coupled with Medicaid or Medicare.

Legend:
A = Always
S = Sometimes

pay after being victimized. Many, for example, completely exclude rehabilitation costs, and limit reimbursement for lost work time to that lost to illness and injury, not time spent with the police or in court.

Gilbert, Specht, and Terrell (1993) offer an alternative view of categories of needs. They characterize "attributed need," in which eligibility is conditional upon belonging to a category or group of people having common needs that are not being met by existing arrangements in the economic market; "diagnostic need," which is based on a medical or mental health diagnosis; and "means-tested need," which is based on a general lack of resources. A fourth category is identified as "compensatory need," which they define as "eligibility conditional upon belonging to certain categories or groups of people who have suffered unmerited disservices at the 'hands of society.'" This suggests that, when *compensation* is the goal of a benefit program, other forms of determining eligibility are redundant. It is interesting to note that, since most so-called compensation programs pay only out-of-pocket costs (denying benefits to people covered by private insurance, for example) and often means-test their benefits, they are *not* compensation programs as Gilbert et al. (1993) define them.

It is also necessary to separate the concept of *substantive* needs, for such items as food, safe shelter, and medical care, from culturally determined or *felt* needs, better defined as desires or expectations. In fact, Bradshaw (1977) distinguished four types of needs:

> **Normative need** refers to some condition of an individual that falls below a standard held by the community or prescribed by some knowledgeable authority.
> **Felt need** refers to a need that is recognized by the individual in question. It is equated with want . . . and . . . is limited by the individual's awareness of the condition and by the individual's own standard of acceptable functioning.
> **Expressed need** refers to a felt need that has been converted into an attempt by the individual to satisfy or fulfill it.
> **Comparative need** refers to the condition of the individual significantly below the average level of that condition in a group of comparable individuals.

Many forms of victim reimbursement reflect normative need as minimal reimbursement of otherwise unreimbursed medical and funeral costs and lost wages to prescribed maximums. Public benefit programs rarely recognize lost property and pain and suffering as needs, and vary in how they assess what the "community standards" are in determining the limits (maximums) of need.

Felt need is compensated only by civil litigation, those few victim compensation agencies that make payments for pain and suffering, and a handful of restitution programs, the latter of which often have difficulty collecting these payments from offenders. Felt needs are entirely subjective, and therefore it is hardly equitable to provide compensation based on felt needs, if only because some victims are unaware of possibilities for meeting them while others have unrealistic expectations that are unrelated to what they might have a right to under the law.

Expressed need is often interpreted by victims or victim service providers. The former may have no sense of what compensation law allows, and the latter may view the services they provide as the ones most necessary to victims, even if this only reflects their narrow view of the situation.

Comparative need is relative to other comparable individuals. This concept of need is the most difficult for victim reimbursement mechanisms to satisfy, particularly when victims experience major life changes, such as the loss of a career, as a result of victimization. While various public benefit programs compensate victims up to their funding caps, victims who lose their livelihoods quickly exhaust capped public benefit coverage, and are forced to depend upon meager means-tested benefits if they can not become employed again and have limited private insurance or savings.

Furthermore, even when benefits are provided, weekly maximum benefits may be much less than victims earned. Victims will then have to rely on other benefits to which they may be entitled unless they have significant alternative sources of income or win substantial civil penalties; or, as is more usual, they will have to drastically alter their lifestyles to bring them into line with their lower incomes. It is important to recognize that even if victim compensation is "fair" in reimbursing victims similarly, most victims consider their economic status not in relation to other victims, but in relation to people who are similar to them in class, occupation, age, education, and other nonvictim characteristics.

Knudten, et. al. (1976) also identified various costs of victimization. They broke them down into financial costs (e.g., medical bills, lost earnings); time costs (e.g., time lost from work, school, free time); and personal costs (e.g., emotional stress, anxiety about having to face the offender, arranging child care and transportation, and doing without stolen property while it is kept in evidence).

Only some of these costs would be defined as needs by any of the above definitions. Yet such intangibles as lost free time and emotional stress are often reimbursed in civil cases under the rubric of pain and suffering. Miller, Cohen and Wiersema (1996) note the importance to public policy of calculating the intangible as well as the tangible costs of crime. For example, they point out that longer incarceration may seem costly—until the total (tangible and intangible) cost of a subsequent victimization, which can presumably be prevented by lengthening the incarceration of a violent offender, is compared to it.

Another way to define costs is to separate current value from replacement cost. Many private and most social insurance programs cover only the current value of items, not the cost to replace them. This separation hurts the poor disproportionately. In fact, wealthy victims of property crimes sometimes relish the opportunity to replace stolen property to keep abreast of current technology. Often they replace electronics equipment, automobiles, and other similar property before it wears out, so insurance payments serve as "bonuses" toward expenditures that they would have made anyway. Poor victims are often uninsured, or do not have enough money to cover the deductible and the difference between the current value of the stolen item and its replacement cost. Consequently, they are more likely to have to do without a replacement of property stolen from them.

As noted, pain and suffering is rarely compensated by private insurance or public compensation programs. This is due to fear of fraud, the difficulty in assessing claims of mental anguish and determining their causes, and the potential cost of such compensation (Stark and Goldstein 1985) on one hand, and a desire to keep such awards in the civil arena, where awards can be much higher than state programs permit (Spence 1989) on the other.

Many government benefit programs pay counseling fees, because they translate the intangible concept of pain and suffering into the only slightly more tangible concept of counseling. This may also be the case because many victim advocates are mental health practitioners, who either believe this correlation to be accurate, or self-servingly support it regardless of its accuracy (Davis and Henley 1990). However, no one has explored the degree of effectiveness of counseling for victims of crime—or the frequency with which effectiveness is reached in actual cases. Nor has anyone explored how victims who receive payments for pain and suffering use them, or whether victims would prefer (or would benefit from) cash in lieu of counseling benefits as a form of pain and suffering payments. In fact, Miller, Cohen and Wiersema (1996) note that mental health counseling has been the least-studied cost of crime.

A 1988b Department of Justice study showed that the poor are most likely to experience violent victimization and that Latinos, Blacks, renters, and those living in central cities (all variables which correlate with poverty) experience more violent crimes than others. Latinos and Blacks are also most likely to require medical attention when injured and to have high financial losses (Bastian 1990, Whitaker 1990). Non-English-speaking people, and people with physical or mental impairments, also figure disproportionately among the poor (Nelson A. Rockefeller Institute of Government 1989).

Yet the poor also have the least access to alternatives to make up their losses (Knudten et al. 1976, Ziegenhagen 1974), and are least likely to know their rights and options. For example, they can rarely afford private insurance and often do not have insurance benefits provided by employers. Ziegenhagen (1974) found that of victims with medical expenses, 38 percent were not covered by or received no reimbursement from medical insurance sources, and of those victims suffering salary losses, 62 percent were not reimbursed. The poor are also least likely to be aware of their right to sue civilly.

Poor people also often lack basic skills, such as reading and writing ability, which facilitate access to and use of human services (Bendick 1980, Bendick and Cantu 1978). This might explain why many benefit claims are disallowed exclusively because victims fail to supply complete information. Such poor, less educated, and often multi problem clients overload bureaucratic systems, and are often screened out by complex rules that they are unable to negotiate (Galper 1975). Criminality and poverty are also associated in the popular mind (Reiman 1984), so society has less sympathy for poor victims. Finally, some programs may overlook the poor because their service providers are mental health practitioners, whose experience with victims tends to be limited to those victims who use their services. As the poor tend to use mental health services less frequently than do others, many service providers may have less contact with poor victims and may, as a result, be less aware of their needs.

A larger proportion of young, male Latinos, Blacks, and members of certain other minority populations, like the poor, who are over represented among them, are prosecuted and jailed as criminals than members of other races. As a result, members of these groups are often hesitant to participate in a criminal justice system they recognize is far more lenient to white criminals.

In addition, the innocence of members of these groups is more often doubted than that of white victims (Reiman 1984). There is reason to believe, then, that they need particularly aggressive outreach and support to enable them to access victim compensation benefits. Actions to make the criminal justice system more responsive to minority group members accused of crimes are also likely to benefit members of those groups who become crime victims, by making them more willing to participate in that system.

Certain victims, such as immigrants and people with physical or mental handicaps, were involved with social agencies that addressed those issues before the victimization occurred. These clients tend to use those other social agencies to deal with their victimizations. Similarly, many religious people turn to their clergy and congregations for help in crises. These helpers may be sensitive to the concerns of victims, but are often unaware of the existence of victim reimbursement mechanisms.

Many crime victims are eligible for other government benefits instead of or in addition to victim compensation. These benefits usually depend on characteristics of the victim other than those that convey victim status. Human service workers are generally aware of the benefits that affect their clients most often. For example, staffs of battered women's programs are usually familiar with Department of Social Services shelter benefits and Aid to Families with Dependent Children (AFDC), and victim compensation agency staff tend to be familiar with workers' compensation and disability benefits, because they must be deducted from compensation benefits. Workers are less likely, however, to be familiar with benefits that they refer to less often, and even less likely to be familiar with current eligibility criteria for these benefits, because those criteria change frequently.

While social services have proliferated, people often experience difficulty in reaching them. This search is especially difficult for the poor, the ill or injured, and the elderly. As noted, many crime victims have at least one, and often several, of these characteristics.

When resources are located, eligibility criteria and other barriers may obstruct access to services. Inquirers may be shunted from agency to agency, and many are so overwhelmed by such impediments as language barriers, inconvenient hours, and remote locations, that they give up altogether. The barriers, fragmentation, and other inadequacies have prompted one expert to describe our society as "over serviced but underserved" (Levinson 1988).

Lack of awareness of alternative sources of reimbursement is not the only problem created by the plethora of benefits. In some cases, delayed awareness can also be problematic. For example, disability benefits are often not retroactive.

Therefore, people who file late lose benefits, even if their reason for filing late was that they thought they were eligible instead for other benefits, such as workers' compensation or crime victims' compensation.

Finally, few workers are familiar with the factors that establish grounds for civil lawsuits. Most ignore them entirely; and a few routinely refer victims to civil attorneys, which can raise false hopes if their cases are not appropriate. Civil lawsuits offer several advantages to victims who have both grounds for them and someone to sue who has assets. In particular, the burden of proof is less stringent than in criminal cases and sizable awards for pain and suffering can be realized.

It is clear that no one agency or type of victim service provider assesses eligibility for all types of reimbursement alternatives. This is due to the fragmentation and deprofessionalization of service provision that occurred during the 1970s. Prior to that time, assessment for benefit eligibility had been viewed as a professional social work function, with each claimant considered individually, differentially, and holistically (National Association of Social Workers 1979).

Today, agencies are loathe to expend resources to help clients who fall outside of their narrow purviews.[1] This results in a conflict between agencies' limited service goals and the profession's relatively unlimited commitments, which is one reason that a relatively small proportion of professional social workers are now found in public assistance agencies (Gummer 1990). But it also points to the need for government agencies to hire some staff members with a broader exposure to human needs and the services available to meet them. Furthermore, these staff members need cross-disciplinary training to learn when and how to refer their clients to other professionals, particularly attorneys.

It appears, then, that many of the neediest victims are unaware of their rights and options, and that even if they were aware of them, many victims might be unable to access these rights without assistance. Shapland (1986), concluded that 57 to 64 percent of victims were not aware of the existence of compensation to which they were entitled. However, Ziegenhagen (1974) found that not all crime victims perceive themselves to be in need of services, and Separovic (1985) found that the majority of crimes do not result in serious loss or injury. Harris (1984) reported that only 19 percent of crime victims were physically injured, and that 26 percent of injured victims did not seek medical attention for their injuries. The United States Department of Justice (1988b) concluded that as few as 10 to 13 percent of violent crime victims incur medical expenses or lose time from work, and two-thirds of them are covered by private insurance or some form of public medical assistance. Jones (1979) documented that fully 68 percent of rape victims, 74 percent of aggravated assault victims, and 77 percent of robbery victims had insurance to meet their medical costs, and that only 22 percent of violent crime victims lost any time from work. These facts suggest that many victims have ample alternative coverage and therefore do not have to rely on public victim reimbursement programs.

Miller, Cohen and Wiersema (1996) estimated the tangible and intangible costs of crime to victims in dollar values. They estimated that victimizations generated $105 billion each year in medical, property, and productivity costs. Pain and suffering costs raised that figure to $450 billion. Furthermore, while each murder generated $2,940,000 in average tangible and intangible costs, rapes, because they were more frequent, were the costliest crimes, resulting in $127 billion in total costs annually.

Carlson (1992) estimated the number of people eligible for crime victim compensation. Using data on crimes generally eligible for compensation, obtained from the Uniform Crime Reports, National Crime Survey, and Fatal Accident Reporting System, he estimated that at least 675,109 violent crimes occurred in 1987. (Violent crimes are the only crimes compensated by most state compensation agencies.) He then deducted unreported crimes and an estimated number of cases in which victims contributed to their injuries (making them ineligible for compensation), and reduced that number by two-thirds to account for victims who had private insurance coverage. Carlson determined that 168,424 crime victims were eligible for victim compensation in 1987. This figure suggests that as many as 22 percent of eligible victims are being served by these programs alone.

While these are the best estimates yet available, they are still imprecise. Contribution is difficult to assess, and, in fact, cannot always be assessed accurately because of insufficient information. Furthermore, some states deny awards because of deemed contribution while others only reduce them (see Chapter 6). Therefore, any guess of the frequency of contribution must be imperfect. Then, too, some victims obtain benefits from multiple sources, so eligibility for one benefit does not automatically preclude use of others.

Even more significant, because the poor are victimized more frequently and more severely than others in the population (United States Department of Justice 1988), more than one-third of crime victims (as opposed to one-third of the general population) are likely to lack insurance coverage. Ziegenhagen (1974) found that 38 percent of crime victims lacked insurance. Increases in unemployment and reductions in medical benefits since Ziegenhagen's and Carlson's studies were conducted have no doubt increased the number of people who lack medical coverage, but that number is undeterminable.

Individuals who sustain small losses may prefer to absorb them rather than go to the trouble of filing a claim (Dulberg 1978). In addition, many victim services were developed to increase reporting crimes to the police, but the majority of victims—and fully 90 percent of victims who had previously reported a crime—felt that the best way to "cut their losses" (Elias 1983) was to avoid the criminal justice process altogether (Hindelang and Gottfredson 1986, Elias 1983, Kidd and Chayet 1984), averting the need for services which advocate with the criminal justice system.

Yet it is still unclear to what extent victims who need and want services receive them. It is also unclear whether unmet needs are caused by lack of awareness of help, lack of eligibility for desired help, lack of belief that help will be forthcoming, lack of skill in obtaining help, lack of access to helpers skilled in providing and obtaining help, or a combination of these factors. Least clear is whether avoidance or ignorance of benefits is exacerbated by reactions to victimization. It is unclear whether reactions such as post traumatic stress disorder, the most common mental health diagnosis attributed to victims, are relatively uncommon, but appear disproportionately in the small proportion of crime victims who seek the help of victim-specific services. Even without data on these issues, however, it is obvious that the more quickly and directly that help is provided to victims, the less they will suffer from additional stress concerning whether they will be reimbursed and how they will meet their economic needs.

Finally, it must be noted that it is impossible to restore people who have been victimized to their former states, in part because those former states were likely to have been characterized by an unrealistically inflated sense of safety. Furthermore, money alone cannot undo the experience of victimization. As the 1982 *Final Report* of the President's Task Force on Victims of Crime noted,

No amount of money can erase the tragedy and trauma imposed on [victims]; however, some financial redress can be an important first step in helping people begin the often lengthy process of recovery. For some, this modest financial assistance can be the lifeline that preserves not only some modicum of stability and dignity but also life itself. (United States Department of Justice 1982)

From this discussion of victim needs, it is clear that the U.S. government is increasingly providing benefits to some victims of crime who could not otherwise meet their costs. However, there is no consensus on the degree to which victim needs should be met by government. Nor is there consensus regarding which victim needs should be met, by what mechanisms, and under what circumstances. This lack of consensus results in enormous disparities in treatment of different victims depending upon the entity responsible for reimbursing them and specifics of the crimes against them—and adds to the confusion over benefit availability.

RATIONALES FOR GOVERNMENT-FUNDED CRIME VICTIM REIMBURSEMENT

Many rationales exist for governments to reimburse victims. Elias (1983) enumerates the following:

> **Strict Liability Theory** proposes that the government owes reimbursement to the victim for having broken its social contract guaranteeing to protect citizens from crime.
> **Government Negligence Theory** is a form of the above limited to crimes which resulted from the negligence of law enforcement personnel.
> **Equal Protection Theory** maintains that government reimbursement is a way in which the risk of crime can be equalized among all potential victims.
> **Humanitarian Theory** places no blame or responsibility on government, but grants reimbursement on humanitarian grounds.
> **Social Obligation Theory** proposes that the state use its police powers on behalf of victims to obtain reimbursement from criminals.

Social Welfare Theory is similar to social obligation theory, but is limited to those victims who are in financial need.

Crime Prevention Theory views reimbursement as an incentive for victims to participate more fully in the criminal justice system.

Political Motives Theory supports victim reimbursement because it is politically popular. Not only does this theory win the support of victims, but also of citizens who feel safer because they know of its existence even if they never need it.

While various methods of reimbursing victims have been adopted and expanded in the past four decades, governments have been reticent to acknowledge an obligation to provide it (United States Department of Justice 1990). In fact, most government entities specifically state that reimbursement is provided as a moral or humanitarian response to help victims who cannot afford the costs that result from crime (Stark and Goldstein 1985). Delaware's victim compensation program states this most overtly, noting that,

although there is no personal duty between the State and a private citizen which guarantees protection from criminals, the harshness of the situation is best ameliorated by some from of statutory compensation, an idea not founded on traditional tort liability but out of moral consideration for the victims of society's and government's inherent limitations. (Delaware State Law, Chapter 90, 1994)

New Jersey's program, on the other hand, is unusual in that it acknowledges this responsibility, stating

the State bears some responsibility for the occurrence of violent crimes since government is authorized to provide for the protection of the populace. When this protection falters, government has the responsibility not only to punish the attacker, but also to assist the victim. (New Jersey State Law, Chapter 4B, 1994)

Furthermore, not all policy makers support the concept of government reimbursement to victims. Opponents suggest that it leads to the abandonment of individual responsibility, and recognize that many victims have a precipitating role in the altercations that lead to their victimization (Smith and Freinkel 1988). Opponents also argue that personal savings, private insurance, and income tax deductions adequately meet the needs of most victims, and that social welfare entitlements and need-based services serve the same purpose for poor victims (Elias 1983). Finally, opponents argue that tort laws, which give victims the right to sue assailants and negligent third parties, provide adequate means for victims to receive reimbursement if they require it (Elias 1983). Even Margery Fry (1959), who introduced the concept of victim compensation in Great Britain, noted the difficulties inherent in those cases that do not result in an arrest or conviction, when a victim's claim can not be objectively confirmed.

Yet one reason that has *not* been advanced in theory was the strongest motivation for developing crime victim compensation abroad. That is, that providing compensation to crime victims as a right, or incorporating it as an eligibility factor in a single-payer health care system, is cheaper and more efficient than tort systems and the fraud prevention mechanisms necessary if health benefits are not provided universally. For example, a young man in New York City, who fell from a window while being chased by police, originally reported that he had been pushed. Later, he admitted that he had been told to say that by onlookers who feared that he would otherwise be unable to meet the medical costs his fall had engendered (Onishi 1995).

Conceptually, reimbursement of crime victims is the easiest public benefit to justify—yet this is only true when it serves as direct redistribution of funds from particular offenders to their specific victims. This is one reason that state crime victim compensation programs have increasingly derived their funds from offender fines. However, taking a step closer to direct redistribution solves one historic problem (what to do when the offender is not caught or is indigent) but creates new ones (how to objectively determine victims' claims and how to justify this redistribution).

The latter concern did not present much difficulty over the past three decades, because redistribution of income was becoming widespread during that time. Today, this issue is being raised once again—in part because of increasing opposition to redistribution, but also because offender funds are being sought to pay a larger range of expenses (such as prison costs) that were formerly funded by tax dollars. The latter can be perceived as siphoning money from victims—or acknowledging that society as a whole is victimized when crimes occur.

Furthermore, there is increasing concern that the provision of benefits undermines responsibility in fundamental ways. Aharoni (1981) has posited that people may take greater risks when they know that those risks have no economic consequences. Service providers may also overtreat or overuse treatment paid for by third parties (Pinkerton 1995, Valente 1995). Most significant, there may be less emphasis on determining the causes of crime and preventing them if the costs of crimes to victims are routinely compensated.

FORMS OF CRIME VICTIM REIMBURSEMENT

Harland (1978) identified seven terms for types of government reimbursement to victims of crime:

> **Restitution** can be used as a general term for all such reimbursement, but is usually limited to goods or their proceeds which are returned to victims upon the conviction of offenders.
>
> **Composition** is an antiquated term for sums of money given to victims by offenders as satisfaction for wrongs.
>
> **Reparation** is generally used in reference to victims of military conflicts.
>
> **Restoration** has the literal sense of returning victims to their former (pre-crime) states.

Indemnification refers to payment owed for action already taken. It is used when private property is taken for public use as well as to refer to the concept that offenders obligate themselves to reimburse victims by their criminal acts.

Compensation denotes **state-funded** or **public reimbursements** to victims.

Community service or service restitution refers to methods by which offenders "work off" their debts to collective victims, such as whole groups, communities or societies, to "undo" the damage they caused (by cleaning graffiti from subway cars, for example); perform service for a not-for-profit or public program related to their crime (such as when those convicted of driving while intoxicated work in emergency rooms or morgues); or do more generalized charitable work.

Of these, compensation will be further discussed in Chapter 6, and restitution and service restitution will be further discussed in Chapter 2. Reparation is only discussed tangentially in this text, because the scope of the text is limited to domestic compensation mechanisms, and discussions of restoration and indemnification will be limited to conceptual analyzes (particularly in Chapters 5 and 7, respectively) of their roles in the reimbursement process.

Nader and Combs-Schilling (1977) analyzed a cross-section of ethnographic examples of victim reimbursement. Based on these examples, they concluded that all share the same functions and purposes: prevention, rehabilitation, restitution, the restatement of values, socialization, regulation, and deterrence. However, how—and how well—each purpose is achieved varies with the specifics of the reimbursement mechanism as well as the specific circumstances of each victimization.

SUMMARY

This chapter introduced the reasons that crime victims require reimbursement, rationales for reimbursing them, the forms that reimbursement can take, and the reasons that reimbursement may be inadequate, or may fail to reach eligible victims. Subsequent chapters will explore each reimbursement mechanism in greater detail. The conclusion of the text will explore recommendations for improving the ways in which victims are compensated for the costs they are forced to incur as a result of crimes committed against them.

NOTE

1. Several reasons have been suggested for this. Piven and Cloward, (1993) and Dulberg (1978) have suggested that this is a way of discouraging "uptake" of benefits. In addition, training workers to determine only one form of entitlement eligibility cuts training costs and makes workers less able to transport their skills to other agencies. These cost savings are offset, however, by the costs created by claimants who put off medical and mental health treatment because they are unable to pay for them, as well as by the financial

costs—often borne by public agencies—of evictions, foreclosures, and bankruptcies, and opportunities lost to claimants as they wade through the morass of bureaucracy.

2

Victim Restitution

Restitution is without a doubt the best option for meeting the needs of crime victims, because it is the fairest means of allocating costs appropriately, as it redistributes funds from offenders directly to the people whom they victimized. Restitution can be therapeutic to both the victim and the offender, and may even serve to reconcile them after the crime. Despite its theoretical effectiveness, however, restitution falls short of meeting most victims' needs for a variety of reasons. These will be explored in this chapter, with suggestions for improving restitution provision and collection.

THE STATE OF THE ART OF VICTIM RESTITUTION

Historically, restitution was the only form of reimbursement available to victims, and it was always paid by the offender and the offender's family to the victim and the victim's family (Jacob 1977). Restitution has been conceptualized as punishment, rehabilitation, and a combination of the two (Barnett and Hagel 1977).

Alternative sentencing, sometimes called community service or service restitution, has become the newest form of restitution (Eglash 1977). One of the benefits of alternative sentencing is that it costs approximately one-tenth of the cost of incarceration (Nassau County Community Services Agency 1989). And, regardless of its type, restitution has been found to significantly reduce recidivism among juvenile offenders (United States Department of Justice 1992), suggesting that its early and consistent use could contribute to crime reduction.

While every state has at least one statute regarding restitution (Sunny von Bulow Victim Advocacy Center 1987), the states vary in how, and how frequently, they make use of it (Sobieski 1991). Table 2.1 identifies the circumstances under which restitution is mandated in each of the states. It shows that 23 states generally mandate restitution, while 16 states mandate it as a condition of probation, 8 as a condition of parole, and 14 in other cases, such as with suspended sentences or work release programs. It should be noted, too, that because setting and collecting restitution are roles of the criminal justice system, which prosecutes crimes in the jurisdiction of occurrence, the rules of the state in which the crime is committed (which may not be the home state of the victim) will dictate the circumstances under which restitution is ordered and collected.

Probation departments are usually responsible for administering restitution orders and collecting payments (Sunny von Bulow Victim Advocacy Center 1987). This adds the weight of law to the restitution process—but also burdens already overloaded agencies with additional, diverse tasks for which they may not be trained. The added fact that probation departments are "offender oriented" suggests that they may not be the ideal locus for restitution collection. In particular, probation officers who relate strongly to their probationers (or the probationers' family members) may underreport probationers' ability to compensate their victims.

The United States Supreme Court has ruled that restitution cannot be discharged in bankruptcy proceedings (Sunny von Bulow Victim Advocacy Center 1987), making it appear to be a reliable form of payment. And it can be generous, because it can incorporate payments for pain and suffering (Sunny von Bulow Victim Advocacy Center 1987) as well as reimbursement for out-of-pocket expenses. It is also the only form of government reimbursement from which victims can expect significant property replacement.

However, these characteristics are tempered by the fact that restitution orders are only as effective as their collection mechanisms, and cannot exceed offenders' ability to pay them. Therefore, many victims fail to receive restitution, even if it has been ordered, and many victims who do receive restitution still require other funds to meet all of the needs caused by the crimes against them. The Victim's Assistance Legal Organization (VALOR) (1996) has identified lack of coordination among the numerous agencies that handle aspects of the restitution process (probation departments, district attorneys' offices, victim witness programs, defense attorneys, and court clerks) as a major impediment to effective restitution collection. Restitution has also been undermined by increased imprisonment and mandatory sentences (Elias 1993).

Victim-offender reconciliation and mediation programs are alternatives to traditional criminal punishment mechanisms that often incorporate restitution. These have the added component of "reconciling" not only financial accounts, but emotional ones, as well. They are especially effective when the victim knows the perpetrator, and is therefore reluctant to engage in an adversarial process, as well as when fault is shared.

Reconciliation is diametrically opposed to our present criminal justice system. Reconciliation seeks to allocate and mitigate blame so both parties can heal and avoid future harm. In doing so, it rewards admissions of guilt, apologies, and remorse.

Table 2.1
States that Mandate Restitution
(and the circumstances under which they do)

STATE	GENERAL	PROBATION	PAROLE	OTHER
Alabama			X	X
Alaska	X			
Arizona	X	X	X	X
Arkansas	X			X
California	X	X		X
Colorado		X	X	X
Connecticut				
Delaware	X			X
Florida	X	X		
Georgia				
Hawaii	X			
Idaho	X			
Illinois				
Indiana				
Iowa	X	X	X	X
Kansas	X	X	X	
Kentucky	X	X		X
Louisiana	X			
Maine	X			X
Maryland				
Massachusetts				
Michigan	X			
Minnesota				
Mississippi				
Missouri				
Montana				
Nebraska				
Nevada	X	X		
New Hampshire				
New Jersey				
New Mexico	X	X	X	
New York	X			X
N. Carolina				X
N. Dakota	X			
Ohio				
Oklahoma				
Oregon				
Pennsylvania				
Rhode Island				
S. Carolina		X		X
S. Dakota				
Tennessee	X	X		X
Texas	X	X	X	
Utah	X	X	X	X
Vermont	X			
Virginia	X	X		
Washington				
W. Virginia				
Wisconsin		X		
Wyoming		X		

Note: Data obtained from Sobieski (1991) and the United States Department of Justice 1984b.

Conversely, the criminal justice system has evolved so that denial of guilt is necessary in order to "win" a case. In criminal cases, too, victims' financial needs are virtually ignored (Dooley 1995).

Another alternative to traditional punishment is restorative justice. This model prioritizes reimbursement to the victim and the community over other forms of punishment, and is generally reserved for nonviolent offenders (Carey 1995).

McGillis (1986) found that four models of restitution practice exist, based on the auspices in which the programs are located. These models are:

> **Restitution as a component of victim/witness assistance programs**, in which restitution is viewed as a victim service and provided within a broader framework of victim services.
>
> **Restitution practiced through victim-offender reconciliation projects**, in which the restitution process itself is a vehicle for addressing the psychological as well as the financial burden of victimization.
>
> **Restitution administered in conjunction with offender supervision provided by probation or parole services**, a low-cost model that adds restitution services to the responsibilities of existing probation staff.
>
> **Restitution administered through court-based employment programs**, which focuses on providing a means of paying restitution as well as collecting it.

While these demonstrate the range of uses of restitution, they also point to its limits—all of these goals are worth pursuing in any single restitution program.

Restitution has many merits: it relieves prison overcrowding (when it is used traditionally, that is, in lieu of prison rather than in addition to it) (Garofalo 1975); it places the burden of compensating the victim on the offender (Barnett and Hagel 1977); and it arguably offers treatment benefits to both the victim and the offender (Goldstein 1974). However, these are theoretical advantages; the use of restitution is far more problematic in practice.

LIMITATIONS OF RESTITUTION

While restitution is, theoretically, the ideal form of both punishment and restoration, it is imperfect in reality. That is because the majority of offenders are never caught or convicted; many offenders who are convicted are indigent, not mentally competent to work, or are simply unwilling to make restitution payments; and poor collection methods fail to collect most of the restitution that is ordered by the courts (Galaway and Hudson 1981). For example, in 1994, restitution was ordered from only 32 percent of the offenders convicted of violent crimes (Maguire and Pastore 1994). Sometimes, too, restitution is a condition of parole, but parole violation or subsequent crimes lead to reincarceration. And even when it is both ordered and received, restitution rarely arrives in time to actually help with the costs for which it was intended (Elias 1983).

Requiring restitution to be paid while the offender is in prison is fraught with further problems. A substantial raise in prison wages would be necessary in any system requiring restitution to be paid by incarcerated offenders. In the United States, businesses have opposed this as unfair competition, and labor unions view it as potentially reducing jobs (Jacob 1977). Therefore, prison labor has been seriously curtailed since the Great Depression.

This has been changing recently, however. In fact, in 1991 the AFL-CIO issued a statement supporting prison labor—if it meets the following conditions:

- It must train prisoners for the jobs available to them upon release.
- It must produce goods and services only for government use, not for sale to the public.
- It must pay prevailing wages for similar work.
- The costs of prisoners' room and board, taxes, restitution and the support of their families should be deducted from prisoners' pay.
- Prisoners should not be used as strikebreakers.
- Prison jobs should not replace jobs in the private sector (AFL-CIO Executive Council on Prison Labor Programs 1991).

Opposition to prison labor continues, but, as states search for ways to reduce the costs of government, more and more are considering charging prisoners (from their prison wages as well as from their personal funds) for room, board, and medical care. If these proposals are effected, they will substantially increase the funds available from prisoners. At the same time, however, they may result in further limits to the funds available to victims for restitution. This is suggested by the fact that, between 1979 and 1992, federal inmates in prison work programs earned a total of $28,668,450; but deductions to their wages totaled only 41 percent, with the largest proportion of deductions, 18 percent, going to pay for their incarcerations, 11 percent for taxes, 7 percent for payments to the prisoners' families, and the smallest portion, 6 percent, allocated for compensating their victims (United States Department of Justice 1995b). It must also be noted, however, that unpaid fines, fees, and costs of incarceration must be absorbed by society, making all taxpayers indirect victims of crime.

A study conducted jointly by the New York State Division of Criminal Justice Services and the New York State Crime Victims Board (1988) found that many victims elect not to request restitution because they have received or are eligible for victim compensation, which tends to be more timely, more certain, and keyed to victims' needs. Furthermore, the bulk of crimes are committed by criminals while they are young (Wilson 1975), so it is no surprise that so many are indigent, and only a handful of states make parents responsible for restitution ordered from minors. However, no studies have attempted to track criminals to determine how many would be able to pay restitution later if these costs followed them throughout their lives as child support, debts to the IRS and student loans increasingly do.

This suggests that restitution may be appropriate in more cases than are currently realized, and that practice, rather than policy, is the cause of its underuse. Additional evidence that restitution can be used more frequently than it currently is used in most states is that Vermont, which mandated reparations in all criminal offenses in its state constitution in 1791 (Dooley 1995), was the last state to develop a victim compensation agency.

OPTIONS FOR IMPROVING RESTITUTION

In sum, for restitution to be effective:

- Law enforcement officers must apprehend a much larger proportion of offenders, and ensure that these offenders are convicted.
- Restitution money must be "advanced" by an agency which can later be reimbursed when the offender is able to pay it.
- Restitution collection methods must be improved, perhaps "flagging" tax returns and state lottery winnings, as is done with child support enforcement, and must include methods of reimbursing third-parties who have already reimbursed victims.
- Inmates must receive significant wages, which can be garnisheed for restitution purposes.
- Restitution must be ordered in every case where it can conceivably be collected.
- Restitution must be keyed to the costs of the victimization.
- State guidelines must be developed to ensure that restitution frequency and levels are uniform.
- The criminal justice system must be reoriented from its "win-lose" perspective to one of mediation and reconciliation, in at least some cases.

Vermont streamlined its restitution system in 1994 by ordering that restitution that compensates victims already reimbursed by that state's victim compensation program be automatically forwarded to the state program. And California regularly publishes a "Restitution Review" newsletter that provides information on restitution and commends those judges who have ordered the most substantial fines ("Vermont Authorizes Restitution to Compensation" 1994).

Victim compensation programs might be required to present reports at sentencing outlining victims' costs, so restitution orders could be keyed to actual expenditures more precisely. Victims who are ineligible for restitution through no fault of their own could be reimbursed at the same level, with their reimbursements paid from a pool of fines or restitution overages. This is not very different from the current trend toward funding compensation programs from offender fees and fines. For this plan to be effective, however, better methods of collection should be developed, and victims who are eligible for restitution should be provided with compensation as soon as the money is needed, with compensation programs bearing the responsibility for collecting restitution when it becomes available.

Restitution should be the ideal method of compensating victims. However, restitution fails when offenders are not apprehended, are not convicted, or are indigent. In any case, restitution is generally not ordered until conviction, and may be provided in payments spread over time. Therefore, it is not an effective way of helping victims meet their costs, but can be a way of reimbursing other benefit providers who have helped victims meet their costs in a more timely way.

Furthermore, restitution could be improved if methods of apprehending and convicting criminals, performing and paying for prison labor, determining indigence, and collecting restitution from the nonindigent were improved. One factor that may facilitate this is the increased use of telecommunications in work situations. In theory, some offenders should be able to bring their work to prison via telecommunication, lessening the need for corrections departments to find jobs for all inmates and enabling some workers to earn more than prison wages. This has yet to be tested, although some prisons currently provide telecommunication work for their prisoners. These include the South Ventura, California Youth Facility, which operates TWA's reservation operation. But this very system exemplifies the problems as well as the advantages of prison labor— the program was set up to counter a TWA strike (Parenti 1995).

Conversely, restitution availability might be improved if more criminals were permitted to serve alternative sentences. DiMascio (1995) identified escalating punishments, including probation, intensive probation, community service, day reporting, house arrest, and electronic monitoring and halfway houses, as methods used to punish criminals without incarceration. While these may not be appropriate for violent criminals or nonviolent recidivist criminals, they increase the possibility that some offenders can remain employed at their regular jobs, making it easier for them to pay restitution.

During the debate on how to improve the collection of cash restitution, some innovators have tried more unusual methods. A judge in Memphis allows victims of property crimes to go to the home of the offender, under guard, to select their choice of the offender's possessions. In one such case, a victim found satisfaction in destroying a photograph of the offender's girlfriend.

SUMMARY

Restitution has many advantages over more recently developed methods of crime victim reimbursement. However, it does not meet the needs of most victims and helps almost none in a timely way.

Other benefits will continue to be necessary if most victims' needs are to be met effectively. Yet restitution should still be used in every case in which it possibly can be—and the possibilities should be expanded as greatly as possible.

3

Private Insurance

Private insurance payments to victims of crime amount to $45 billion annually, including over $13 billion in property coverage (Miller, Cohen and Wiersema 1996), most of which would not be reimbursable through government programs. Private insurance meets the needs of crime victims in two ways: it meets the expenses of people who are themselves insured against the costs of crime, and in some cases it covers the expenses of people injured in places (or by automobiles) that are covered by private insurance.

Private insurance is also the source of certain government benefits, notably workers' compensation. However, because the regulatory structures of these mandated benefits more closely resemble government benefits, they will be discussed in Chapter 4.

Crime victims must negotiate, and often sue, to obtain coverage under the insurance policies of others (although most such lawsuits are settled before they reach the courtroom). Therefore, there is usually considerable delay in obtaining these benefits, and victims will need to seek alternative means of meeting their costs while waiting for settlements or the outcome of court cases.

On the other hand, personal insurance coverage has many advantages as a means of covering losses due to crimes, including its almost immediate availability and its relatively uncomplicated nature (Mueller and Cooper 1975). Its main disadvantage is cost: the poorest victims can neither afford private insurance nor absorb the high deductibles involved with lower-cost insurance.

An increasingly troublesome disadvantage is that insurers have been, during the past two decades in particular, reducing coverage as an additional means of cost containment at the same time that they have been drastically increasing premiums. This has not only resulted in losses of coverage, but in denials of coverage to people who have paid for insurance and believe that they are entitled to coverage (Guarino and Trubo 1974).

THE STATE OF THE ART OF PRIVATE CRIME INSURANCE

There are five major types of private insurance available to offset the costs of crime to victims.

Automobile Insurance

This is the type of private insurance that is most nearly universally carried. Near-universal coverage is possible because ownership of an automobile is in itself a luxury; the government therefore can restrict ownership to people who carry insurance coverage without denying basic rights.

Private automobile insurance pays $23.5 billion annually in coverage to victims of crime (Miller, Cohen and Wiersema 1996). If victims are injured by uninsured vehicles, pooled funds from insurance carriers are generally available to meet their costs. Automobile insurance policies usually cover theft of vehicles as well as fire and vandalism of vehicles. It generally does not cover theft of property from vehicles, which may be covered, instead, by homeowners' or other property insurance.

In some states, intentional injuries with automobiles are specifically excluded from coverage under automobile insurance regulations. However, in 1994 the New Jersey Supreme Court ruled that the victim of a drive-by shooting could collect benefits under his father's no-fault policy. This decision was particularly significant because the injury was not even caused by the automobile itself, but by a passenger in it (Sullivan 1994).

Still, states differ in how they interpret these cases, and often each case is determined in a somewhat different manner. Victims should consider the availability and applicability of automobile insurance to meet crime-induced costs, but should understand that they can not assume that they will be covered for all circumstances under every policy or in every location.

Life Insurance

According to the American Council on Life Insurance, 62 percent of the population is covered by life insurance. Information on costs and amounts of coverage varies, but it can be assumed that not all of those covered by life insurance have coverage adequate to support their dependents when they die without additional income from other sources. In fact, instead of supporting family members after a death, life insurance is often adequate only to cover the costs of a funeral and burial. This is also suggested by the fact that life insurance payments based on crimes add up to only $1.5 billion annually, significantly less than the $11 billion annually paid by insurance companies for medical payments, the $7.9 billion paid on homeowners' claims, or the $23.5 billion paid on crimes covered by automobile insurance (Miller, Cohen and Wiersema 1996).

Property Insurance

Little specific information is available about property insurance coverage. It is impossible to determine how much property is currently uninsured, because there is no way to determine the amount of insurable property in existence. Again, too, the poor are more likely to have property stolen from them, but are less likely to have that property covered by insurance.

When property is stolen, private insurers often do not pay full value, if they pay at all. Property insurance rules both discount original costs (citing depreciation and "wear and tear") and limit payments if property was not properly secured. For these reasons, "replacement value" property insurance has become the most common form of property insurance. Those who choose not to purchase, or cannot afford, replacement value coverage may not receive sufficient reimbursement to repurchase items lost through theft, vandalism, or arson.

Homeowners' Insurance

This is a specific type of "comprehensive" coverage that incorporates property, health, casualty, and even life insurance in a single policy covering a particular residential location. As noted, crime-related claims against homeowners' insurance amount to $7.9 billion annually (Miller, Cohen and Wiersema 1996).

As homeowners' policies cover injuries that occur on the premises (and sometimes cover injuries to insured parties off the premises), crime victims, including battered spouses and children, have attempted to collect against them if they were injured in the offender's home. (Refer to a further discussion of this concept in Chapter 5.) Homeowners' policies generally exclude "named insureds" who live on the premises, however. This automatically excludes spouses and children who live on the premises from coverage under policies which cover their own residences. As with automobile insurance, insurers and courts have differed in how they interpret these policies. Particularly at issue is the question of whether intentional injuries are covered under policies based on negligence, or whether negligence coverage under such policies is limited to accidental injuries.

Health and Casualty Insurance

Health and casualty insurance rates have risen at twice the rate of inflation for the past 20 years. As a result, many employers, who have always been the primary insurers of nonelderly Americans, have cut back on the health care benefits they provide to employees. Employers have also increased their use of part-time and temporary workers, most of whom are not eligible for benefits of any kind. It was estimated that 38.5 million nonelderly Americans lacked both private and publicly financed health care coverage in 1992 (Cutler 1994).

This number triples when ability to pay for health services is calculated, because many health insurance plans have such high deductibles and low maximums that people covered by them still have unreimbursed medical bills after they have exhausted the insurance coverage available to them. This is true despite the existence of the Medicaid and Medicare systems, which many presume are a safety net for people who are not covered by private insurance programs. Those without health insurance generally earn too much money to be eligible for Medicaid, are too young to obtain Medicare, do not work for an employer who provides health insurance, work part-time for an employer who covers only full-time workers, cannot afford private health insurance, are not covered under a parent's or spouse's plan, or suffer from an illness or disability that makes them ineligible for coverage related to their preexisting condition.

Partners in gay and lesbian relationships may be disproportionately denied health benefits under partners' plans, although domestic partnership plans (for heterosexual as well as homosexual couples) are becoming increasingly available. It is unclear how many such partners lack coverage of their own; nor is it clear whether some partners would be unwilling to disclose their homosexuality to qualify for these benefits if they were available.

Even when offered the option, most employees are unable or unwilling to bear a greater portion of their health care costs than they currently pay. Therefore, service cutbacks have become common. Some employers pay flat fees to health maintenance organizations, which then limit patient services to ensure profits. Health maintenance organizations ration health care by limiting the number of doctor visits, hospital days, or amounts of other resources available to those insured. In some cases, patients cannot use services until they have been approved by an insurance company "care manager."

Some Americans are virtually prohibited from obtaining private health insurance. Those with preexisting conditions find it difficult to obtain coverage at any price.

Still others are unable to afford such coverage. And this is not limited to "the poor," who are generally eligible for public benefits. Because health care is generally provided by employers, the unemployed lose benefits along with their jobs. Similarly, those who are permanently injured may become eligible for benefits based upon their injuries, but lose other health care, along with coverage for family members. Finally, when employees retire before the age of 65, they and their spouses under 65 lose all medical benefits until they become eligible for Medicare at 65.

Government regulations require that employment-linked health insurance plans offer extended coverage to former employees who have ceased employment for any reason. These plans, enacted under the Consolidated Omnibus Budget Reconciliation Act of 1985 (COBRA), were designed to tide employees over for up to 18 months while they are moving between jobs (COBRA 1995). But people forced from employment due to disability do not always become employed again, and are often unable to pay the premiums that would enable their insurance to continue.

It should be noted that some of the limitations of health care services actually protect the public from unnecessary medical procedures. This can be particularly effective when "care managers" have health care training. However, few do, and when health care is limited due to costs rather than lack of need, it often creates excessive costs farther down the line, which generally must be met by the public sector. Even so, private health insurance covers $11 billion in victim claims annually (Miller, Cohen and Wiersema 1996).

LIMITATIONS OF PRIVATE INSURANCE

All forms of private insurance have limits of various kinds (Mehr and Cammack 1980). Therefore, it is conceivable that any crime victims who are seriously enough injured could exceed the limits of their private insurance coverage.

Automobile insurance policies often become void if the vehicle is used in a crime. In addition, if policy holders are victims of violent crime in their cars, the insurers will usually refuse to pay medical bills or lost earnings because the injuries did not result from an accident.

Life insurance appears inadequate to meet the needs of the families of homicide victims, since 38 percent of the population is uncovered. Furthermore, it is not clear how much life insurance is available to the average insureds, or how many people of what ages are covered by life insurance. It is obvious, however, that few survivors rely on life insurance premiums alone for their incomes (many exhaust these funds paying for the funeral and burial), so these funds can not be adequate for most individuals and families.

Although little is known regarding the extent of property insurance coverage, the federal government had to create subsidized insurance to cover people unable to obtain insurance elsewhere. Therefore, two things can be concluded: not all people can afford private property insurance, and even some who can afford it are unable to obtain it because they live in "redlined" neighborhoods, whose high crime rates make private insurers unwilling to provide them with coverage at any cost. In addition, many renters are not insured for property damage because, while mortgage holders generally insist that mortgagees carry insurance, no such rules exist for either tenants or landlords. The lack of availability of property insurance makes it particularly ironic that government compensation programs rarely cover significant amounts of property loss, particularly when the loss results from nonviolent crimes such as burglary. Homeowners' insurance is often interpreted as not covering crimes committed in private homes because of the intentional nature of these acts.

Health and casualty insurance varies according to the amount of coverage and the degree to which that coverage provides for discrete needs associated with different injuries and illnesses. (The latter might include rehabilitation, pharmaceutical drugs, and medical appliances.) Most people obtain health insurance as an employee benefit, and have limited choice of providers or coverage. Only large employers (if they choose to do so) can offer employees a choice of policies or insurance carriers. Private health insurance coverage, even if it is not health maintenance organization-affiliated, may limit treatment to certain doctors and hospitals—and may rule out payments to foreign health service providers entirely.

This peculiar lack of uniformity in coverage is not unique to crime victims. Consider the insight on the "bizarre priorities" of insurance carriers that journalist John Hockenberry gained during his rehabilitation following an automobile accident:

If we had another identity besides our injury it was the label of our insurance policy. So much was determined by the pattern of insurance coverage. The most confident fully covered folks were the ones injured in car accidents. With the pool of all licensed drivers in America paying for it, insurance companies could afford to be generous. Car accident injuries could expect almost complete medical coverage. . . .

People injured in public places such as playgrounds or swimming pools, where liability was a question, came next. They usually benefitted from the payout of some insurance policy on the facility where they were injured. They also could generally count on some kind of legal settlement if they sued the facility. The next group were those injured at work, who came under workers' compensation. Coverage here was less than for auto accidents, but fairly complete nonetheless.

In considerably worse shape were those people with degenerative conditions that came on suddenly. These people often exhausted their insurance in the first weeks of acute care and had little or nothing left for rehab. . . . They were the recipients of a kind of medical rationing. . . .

This set of medical priorities meant that a drunk driver who lost control of a vehicle, someone whose injury was nearly self-inflicted, received a full ride from the health-care system. But someone whose disability was the result of disease and had occurred through no fault of his own was left out in the cold. (Hockenberry 1995)

OPTIONS FOR IMPROVING CRIME INSURANCE

Automobile insurance is effective as far as it goes, although in some jurisdictions enforcement against uninsured motorists is lax and needs to be improved. Two legislative changes could make automobile insurance more effective in covering crime victims, however. Automobile insurance coverage could be extended to victims of driving while intoxicated, hit-and-run and intentional injuries inflicted by or in automobiles—with draconian penalties for driving without insurance coverage. To ensure that this would not bankrupt insurance companies, penalties for these crimes would have to be increased significantly, as well. These two actions would reinforce each other: insurance companies would be careful not to insure drivers who had been convicted of these crimes, but would charge them high premiums that would force them to be responsible for their actions in their cars or find alternate transportation. As a result, drivers would be less likely to commit these crimes—if the law were enforced effectively.

Life insurance may well be a luxury that many crime victims, and others, manage without. However, life insurance is frequently used to pay for socially desirable activities, such as funding children's advanced educations. Therefore, other government mechanisms, such as student loans and grants, should be reviewed to ensure that they fulfill these needs for people unable to meet them due to crime-caused death or injury.

Property insurance appears to fall into the luxury category with life insurance. However, some limited funds should be made available through crime victim compensation or other benefit agencies to cover essential property, and essential property should then be carefully defined.

Homeowners' insurance might also be extended to cover intentional injuries, but should be prohibitively expensive to people with a history of victimizing others. This would enable it to also serve both a protective and a preventive function. If this is not done, at the very least the concept of negligence should be clarified so potential litigants can determine whether they might collect under a particular policy before initiating a lawsuit. Furthermore, "redlining" should be prohibited, even if the government has to subsidize property insurance coverage in some neighborhoods. (See Chapter 4 for a further discussion of this concept.)

One way to increase private health insurance coverage would be to legalize currently illegal businesses. Illegal businesses, including legal activities which fail to pay taxes as well as illegal activities, do not provide mandatory benefits for employees. Yet illegal gambling and drug sales alone generate over $160 billion annually (Miller, Cohen and Wiersema 1996, "Betting Odds" 1995), and are responsible for far more workplace-centered violence than are legal businesses. Legalizing these businesses would force them to cover their workers under workers' compensation, which would increase those agencies' revenues, free victim compensation programs from having to make decisions about these cases, and preserve public resources for those victims who truly have no other source of reimbursement. Keeping these businesses illegal, on the other hand, further exploits the workers in these fields, while legalization would force employers to adhere to the same employee protection requirements that legal businesses must- or would at least offer employees the strength of law against employers who failed to do so.

Various options for improving health insurance have been proposed in recent years. They range from taxpayer-funded, universal health care to minor "tinkering" with premium caps, large pools that cannot exclude those with preexisting conditions, and tort reforms that would reduce malpractice insurance costs.

All of the industrialized countries of the world, except the United States and South Africa, currently provide health care to their citizens as a right. This reflects a belief that the risk of injuries and illnesses should be shared. These programs have also proven to be far more cost-effective than our highly discriminatory health care system.

The recent experiences of workers' compensation programs, the oldest state and federal benefit programs available to Americans, point to yet another reason for universalization of health benefits: it is becoming more and more difficult to separate work-related causes of injuries and other health problems from other factors which may have contributed to, if not caused, the problems. Early in the development of workers' compensation, most identified workplace injuries were caused by unsafe machinery. Later, dangerous chemicals replaced machinery as primary identified causes of claims, but these were similarly easy to link directly and solely to workplace exposure.

More recently, air contaminants, repetitive motion injuries, emotional stress, and interpersonal violence have become leading causes of workers' compensation claims, but these factors are essentially different from those identified earlier. While air contaminants, repetitive motion injuries, and emotional stress can all be linked to the workplace, workers may be affected differently according to their off-site exposure to conditions that exacerbate them. For example, it is not completely fair to assess an employer for the full cost of surgery for repetitive motion injury to an employee who not only uses a keyboard at work, but plays tennis often during off-work hours.

Furthermore, there is evidence of interaction among these factors. Workplace stress, for example, can cause or exacerbate many medical conditions. How are these costs to be allocated, particularly if one benefit provides more or better coverage?

Interpersonal violence creates yet another circumstance unanticipated when workers' compensation was developed. While employers should, of course, safeguard employees from violence as they do from other hazards, they should not be wholly responsible for the costs of violence to workers, if only because that policy releases offenders from responsibility toward their victims.

For these reasons, since 1991 there has been increasing discussion of 24-hour or wraparound coverage for employees, which would integrate workers' compensation with other benefits at least in cases such as those noted. Under 24-hour coverage, there would be no need to investigate how an injury was sustained, because employees would receive the same benefits for any injury, regardless of where or how it occurred (Singer, Neale, and Schwartz 1987).

This is also the best argument for universal health benefits: health care would not be denied—or delayed—while benefit agencies play "hot potato" with cases. Instead, a single administrative entity, public or private, would approve care according to need alone. Care would then be paid for from a single fund pooled from employers, employees, taxes, offenders, and other sources.

In order to fairly allocate costs, such a single payer system at some point would have to, assess which entities are responsible for which portions of costs, and allocate charges accordingly. Furthermore, it would be imperative that such a system use this information to target prevention efforts to those causes and entities most responsible for the largest number of claims as well as the most costly claims for all types of illnesses and injuries. People who favor the current tiered health care system, which favors the rich and is particularly punitive toward those people who depend on public benefit systems to pay their health care costs, should remember that many victims of violence must rely on these meager benefits.

Yet universal insurance coverage contains the inherent danger that people might be less inclined to avoid dangers when they know that they are fully insured against them (Aharoni 1981). This can be exacerbated if society uses the availability of universal coverage to justify avoiding prevention efforts or making improvements to safety mechanisms. Individuals can be encouraged to take preventive measures or to invest in safety equipment through public education, and discouraged from overusing benefits by the use of deductibles and copayments. But even under universal health care it would still be vital for the government to encourage larger-scale security efforts, ranging from legislation to criminal justice enhancements to conducting research to determine how to reduce victimizations as well as how to compensate them.

SUMMARY

Private crime insurance meets many needs that public benefits do not. Some of these are for "luxuries," which those who cannot afford them must do without, but others cover items and services needed desperately regardless of ability to pay. Furthermore, because of the prohibitive costs of such insurances, many crime victims find themselves without, or with inadequate, private insurance. Until private insurance is available to all, at least to meet those needs considered basic, public benefits of all sorts will be necessary to enable crime victims to meet needs caused by crime that they cannot meet with their own resources.

4

Social Welfare and
Other Government Programs

As noted in the Introduction, many government benefits exist to help people meet needs caused by crime that are not specifically defined as "crime victim benefits," because eligibility for these benefits is based on means tests or other nonvictim characteristics. Therefore, in reviewing them, their other eligibility factors should be carefully noted.

These benefits also differ in terms of how they are financed. Some are contributory (such as OASI), some are private insurance regulated by government (such as workers' compensation) and others, such as AFDC, are funded by general tax revenues.

Many public benefits also have strict filing deadlines. Therefore, it is wise for victims to apply for all benefits potentially available to them as soon as they learn of them. This is true even if they are not certain that they will exhaust their private or other public benefits, because by the time that they do exhaust them, if they do, it may be too late to file for alternatives.

THE STATE OF THE ART OF SOCIAL WELFARE PROGRAMS

The major social welfare benefits and their eligibility criteria follow.[1] Benefit levels that vary by locality have been omitted, as have specifics of assets tests, which should be assumed when the term *economically needy* appears.

Aid to Families With Dependent Children (AFDC)

Economically needy families with dependent children may be eligible for semi-monthly cash payments to meet basic housing and shelter needs. Dependent children are defined as those deprived of support due to the absence, death, incapacitation, or unemployment of a parent. Employable adults generally must work, look for work, or be enrolled in a job training program to be eligible. AFDC is that portion of the "safety net" into which families of crime victims fall when they lose wages due to the death, injury, or unemployment of a worker. Since all compensation programs have a cap, or maximum, on lost wages or support, many families with dependent children who are unable to access other sources of income to make up the financial losses caused by crime must eventually rely on AFDC for support.

Disability (DBL)

Six states (California, Hawaii, Massachusetts, New Jersey, New York, and Rhode Island) mandate disability coverage for workers, and 25 percent of the workforce is covered under one of these programs. An additional two-thirds of the workforce is covered by noncompulsory disability benefits, suggesting that more than 91 percent of full-time workers have access to disability payments of some kind. Workers who have been employed full time for a minimum qualifying period and who are disabled in a non-work-related incident may be eligible for payments.

However, disability benefits can range from minimal subsistence payments to reimbursement of full salary, and the length of time than benefits continue can differ greatly, as well. There is sometimes a lag of several days or weeks before workers become eligible for disability payments. Usually, employees must request disability benefits from their employers; employers are not generally obligated to notify employees at the time of the injury of the existence of these benefits.

As a result, many workers remain ignorant of these benefits. In addition, claims filed late by injured workers may only be paid from the date filed, not from the date of the injury. Workers disabled as the result of a crime may be able to receive disability payments if they are unable to qualify for victim compensation, or if they are still disabled when they reach the compensation wage cap.

Earned Income Tax Credits (EITC)

Taxpayers who are supporting at least one minor or disabled adult child and who earn less than $24,396 in adjusted gross income in a single tax year can receive credits of a proportion of their adjusted gross income, to a maximum of $2094; taxpayers with two children may earn slightly more, and may claim up to $3110.[2] Crime victims who lose income as a result of crime, who suffer significant property loss that reduces their adjusted gross income, or who are simply poor may qualify to receive EITCs.

Emergency Assistance (EA)

People who receive or are eligible for SSI, AFDC, or HR may receive emergency funds to avoid hunger, cold, or unsafe conditions. Victims of arson or theft of such essentials as food, coats, blankets, or money earmarked to purchase these items, who are also receiving or are eligible to receive the entitlements noted, may be issued money or vouchers to cover the costs of these items.

Food Stamps (FS)

Low-income households may receive vouchers with which to purchase food or seeds. Crime victims whose income is reduced temporarily or permanently may be eligible for food stamps to supplement their income.

Hill-Burton Uncompensated Services

In 1946, Congress passed a law guaranteeing grants and loans to hospitals and other health care facilities. Known as the Hill-Burton Act for its primary sponsors, Senators Lister Hill and Harold Burton, the law required that facilities that obtained these funds provide free services to the poor in lieu of repayment to the government. The Department of Health and Human Services publishes a list of Hill-Burton facilities and annually calculates income amounts that make patients eligible for free or reduced-cost services. Facilities can determine which services to cover and do not have to continue providing these services once they have reached their annual caps (United States Department of Health and Human Services 1994).

Home Energy Assistance Program (HEAP)

Recipients of AFDC, HR recipients with children, and SSI recipients who live alone are eligible for one supplemental fuel or utility payment during the heating season. There are additional HEAP benefits for the elderly. Crime often pushes into poverty victims who would otherwise "just get by" financially. HEAP offers a supplemental payment that can help victims "catch up" with bills when crime reduces their income or results in unexpected costs.

Home Relief (HR)

Economically needy adults under 65 who are not disabled may be eligible for semi-monthly payments to meet basic needs. HR is always the last resort for people unable to qualify for other benefits. Payment levels are low, but victims who are ineligible for other benefits may find it their only means of support.

Income Tax Deductions (ITD)

Taxpayers can take deductions for significant losses. Losses must amount to more than 10 percent of the victim's adjusted gross income plus $100 to be deductible (Stark and Goldstein 1985). Victims who sustain large, uncompensated losses, most often caused by fire, theft, or vandalism, may be able to offset some of their losses in this way.

Medicaid[3] (MD)

Recipients of AFDC, HR, and SSI, as well as other economically needy people who are blind, disabled, or elderly, may receive medical, hospital, or long-term care. Others can become eligible if they suffer a catastrophic injury or illness for which they incur large expenses. Victim compensation programs generally do not require victims to apply to Medicaid, but victims who are ineligible for compensation may find it the only way to pay their medical bills.

Medicare (ME)

Recipients of OASI who are over 65, people who have received SSI for more than two years, and people with end-stage renal disease are eligible for insurance that covers up to 80 percent of most "reasonable charges" for physicians, hospital, respite, senior nursing facility, home health, and hospice care. Supplemental Medicare insurance can be purchased at a rate lower than private insurance. Medicare is the primary insurer of most Americans over 65, and pays most of the medical costs of senior victims whether or not they report crime or otherwise comply with compensation program requirements.

Old Age and Survivors' Insurance (OASI)

Workers who have made at least minimal contributions are eligible for benefits based on their contributions when they reach 65; or they can opt for a 20 percent reduction in benefits at 62. If workers die before reaching 65, their surviving spouses and any children under 16 are entitled to survivor benefits. If the children are residing with a spouse who is unemployed, or is employed on a part-time basis receiving a modest yearly income, the spouse, as well as the children, are eligible for benefits. If the deceased was not married at the time of death, survivor benefits may be obtained by anyone who has legal guardianship of any children of the deceased. Surviving spouses become eligible for reduced benefits when workers die, as do divorced spouses who were married for at least 10 years. A burial benefit of $255 is also available for covered workers.

People who are widowed or orphaned as a result of crime and are eligible for OASI payments can rely on these to meet a significant portion of their lost support, and people over 62 who are injured or fearful of crime and would otherwise have continued to work may opt for benefits, as well. These benefits may make them ineligible for victim compensation wage replacement, or may form a base so that compensation benefits can be stretched over a longer period than if they had to provide full support for the recipients.

Railroad Retirement Act (RR)

Federal employees are not covered under the Social Security Act; however, similar survivor benefits are available to them and their survivors under the

Railroad Retirement Act. If the workers also worked in OASI-covered employment, they or any survivors are entitled to both benefits. (See OASI.)

Supplemental Security Income (SSI)

Economically needy blind, disabled, or elderly people are eligible for monthly benefits. Victims who are blinded or disabled as a result of crime may opt for SSI if they fail to qualify for compensation, or to meet their needs when compensation payments are exhausted. SSI can be used to supplement very low OASI and DBL benefits.

Unemployment Insurance (UI)

Workers in covered employment who are unemployed through no fault of their own are entitled to benefits. Workers must have been in covered employment and have earned minimum required amounts before becoming unemployed to be eligible. Benefits are generally exhausted in 26 weeks, although in times of high unemployment benefits are often extended. Victims who lose their jobs because they were injured or had to attend to criminal justice matters may be eligible for unemployment benefits if they fail to qualify for victim compensation to cover their lost earnings, or to meet their needs when compensation payments are exhausted.

Veterans' Benefits (VB)

Veterans who were disabled in the armed services or are financially needy are eligible for free health care in Veterans' Administration hospitals and payments for service-related disabilities. When veterans who received such payments die, their spouses and children may be eligible for survivor benefits. A funeral benefit of $250 is available if the veteran is buried in a national cemetery, or $400 if other funeral arrangements are made. A victim who is an eligible veteran, or such a veteran's survivors, may use VB instead of or in addition to victim compensation to cover medical, burial, and support expenses.

Workers' Compensation (WC)

All employers who have one or more employees are mandated by law to carry workers' compensation insurance. This insurance covers employees from their first day on the job for any accidental injury arising "out of and during the course of employment." Workers' compensation law calls for the payment of all medical expenses causally related to the injury on which the claim is based. A percentage of the worker's gross wages is payable to workers or, if deceased, workers' survivors.

Employers must notify the workers' compensation insurance carrier that workers have been injured or killed on the job. Therefore, claims that are filed late are still paid from the date of the workers' injury or death rather than from the date of filing.

In cases in which employers, in violation of the law, are found not to carry workers' compensation insurance, workers may file a claim with the "No Insurance" section of workers' compensation. A burial benefit is also available for workers whose deaths arose out of and during the course of their employment. Victims who are injured on the job are eligible for both victim compensation and workers' compensation benefits, but they must exhaust workers' compensation first, then may receive victim compensation if workers' compensation does not meet all of their costs.

Most states treat workplace violence like any other workplace injury. But some few states recognize specific aspects of workplace violence, in order to treat it differently. For example, Arkansas' statute specifies that

"Compensable injury" does not include . . . injury to any active participant in assaults or combats which, although . . . in the workplace, are the result of non-employment-related hostility or animus of one, both, or all . . . the combatants, and which said assault or combat amounts to a deviation from customary duties. (Arkansas Workers' Compensation Commission 1993)

This obviously prevents those who commit violence in the workplace from obtaining workers' compensation for violent injuries they initiated. On the other hand, Hawaii's recognition of workplace violence enhances benefits to victims, since an "accident arising out of and in the course of employment includes the wilful act of a third person directed against an employee because of the employee's employment" (Hawaii Department of Labor and Industrial Relations 1993).

This is a particularly important, and unique, feature that ensures that workers targeted because of their employment (in government offices or abortion clinics, for example) are recognized as eligible for workers' compensation even for crimes that occur off the premises of the workplace.

Victims of workplace violence should also note that language defining workers' compensation as an exclusive remedy only limits their options in regard to suing their employers (employers are increasingly being sued, as Chapter 5 will discuss). Nothing prevents victims of workplace violence from suing and collecting from coworkers, customers, or others who were negligent or willfully violent toward them, even if they received workers' compensation payments.

THE STATE OF THE ART OF OTHER GOVERNMENT PROGRAMS

District attorney's offices in many jurisdictions are authorized to make payments to witnesses, whether or not they are victims, for the time they spend in court. District attorney's offices are also empowered to pay for the relocation of witnesses who are endangered as a result of their testimony. However, victims do not appear to be receiving these fees and services to any significant extent. For example, Elias (1983) found that only 2 percent of the victims he studied had received witness fees. Nothing suggests that collection of witness fees has improved since then.

Victim compensation programs specifically exclude payment of lost work time for court appearances, because victims are supposed to receive them from district attorneys' offices. However, since most victims do not receive these fees, the funds to cover them might be transferred from district attorneys' budgets to compensation programs, and the latter empowered to pay them. This is just one of many ways that compensation programs could be used to consolidate services to victims, lessening the number of providers victims must contact to be compensated for their costs and increasing the number of victims whose costs can be fully met.

High costs and redlining by private insurance companies led the federal government to develop lower-cost, no-refusal property insurance coverage for those unable to obtain, or afford, property insurance from private concerns. Federal Crime Insurance is available in only 17 jurisdictions (Alabama, California, Connecticut, Delaware, the District of Columbia, Florida, Georgia, Illinois, Kansas, Maryland, New Jersey, New York, Pennsylvania, Puerto Rico, Rhode Island, Tennessee, and the Virgin Islands), because these areas have the highest rates of urban crime (Federal Emergency Management Administration 1989).

The federal plan protects residential losses up to $10,000 and commercial losses up to $15,000, on the condition that adequate security devices were in place at the time of the crime. Costs are low and coverage is guaranteed, but individuals and businesses must have had the funds, and the foresight, to purchase it before a crime occurs.

The Federal Crime Insurance Program was originally funded by the National Insurance Development Fund, but losses made it necessary for the government to augment the fund with federal money (United States General Accounting Office 1981). These losses have also made the federal government consider ending the Federal Crime Insurance program.

However, lack of property insurance is a persistent problem, which money alone will not solve. Therefore, it is important for the government to continue both supporting subsidized insurance and providing compensation to make up for uninsured losses.

Before closing or altering the Federal Crime Insurance program, an assessment should be made to determine whether similar insurance is now available to its holders at prices they can afford. If it is not, the cost savings of cutting the program would be offset by uninsured losses of businesses that would have to close as a result. These losses would be felt particularly hard in inner cities. An alternative might be to outlaw redlining, although government subsidies might be needed to ensure that people who live in poor neighborhoods could afford insurance if it were made available.

The federal government also developed an arm of the Securities and Exchange Commission that reimburses people who are victims of securities fraud, from a fund created with fines against offenders who commit these crimes (United States Department of Justice 1988a). Four hundred million dollars, or 80 percent of the fine Michael Milken was assessed as a result of his crimes involving junk bonds, went to this fund.

Some states have set up similar programs for victims of other forms of fraud, as well. For example, the New York State Bar Association created a program for people who are treated fraudulently by attorneys, which was funded from assessments against all members (New York State Clients' Security Fund 1987). However, the fragility of this fund was demonstrated when it was bankrupted in 1991 with $30 million in claims left unpaid (Tayler 1992).

From time to time, the government also develops self-limiting programs for victims of particular types of corporate crime, usually as a result of a class-action suit against the firm (see Chapter 5). Makers of the Dalkon Shield and Agent Orange are among the corporations that have had to set up such programs (Mokhiber 1988).

Finally, the government is moving toward paying "class-action" compensation itself. In 1990, the United States finally compensated Japanese-Americans for losses suffered when they were interned in concentration camps here during World War II. However, this compensation was limited to only $20,000 per person ("Restitution Payments" 1990). The government never paid victims of slavery a proposed "forty acres and a mule" to enable them to become self-sufficient after their forced servitude, although some observers have argued that affirmative action and other such targeted programs serve this purpose today (Elden 1970).

A recent attempt at paying class-action compensation in Hungary highlighted the difficulty imposed by delays in making these payments. Although the Hungarian government offered coupons worth the equivalent of up to $67,000 with which former owners could bid on their government-confiscated land, few Hungarians have acted on the offer. Increased mechanization and the loss of agricultural skills over generations have made the return to the farm daunting if not prohibitive ("Auction of Land" 1992).

LIMITATIONS OF SOCIAL WELFARE AND OTHER GOVERNMENT PROGRAMS

As can be seen, each social welfare program has its own eligibility requirements and compensation levels. Many require membership in a particular group, such as that of workers, and are therefore unavailable to many victims. Others require victims to be nearly indigent to collect, and some require a medical diagnosis that precludes work, as well. Many working poor people earn too much money to be entitled to means-tested public assistance, but not enough to absorb a loss due to a crime.

Elias (1983) observed that public assistance programs tend to be demeaning, unreliable, and inequitable. Further, because they are not keyed to inflation, and have not been raised in some time, public assistance benefits are too low to be considered adequate by any measure. They can, however, supplement compensation to form a package that better meets the needs of victims than any one program alone.

It is important to note that this coordination of benefits is assumed by lawmakers, who design new services only to meet those needs unmet by existing services. Therefore, programs that focus on the use of only one program or benefit can rarely meet the needs of victims.

It appears that no other social welfare programs guarantee a range and level of benefits comparable to those of victim compensation programs, particularly for catastrophic medical costs and travel costs for medical and criminal justice purposes. Workers' compensation benefits are often as generous, but are subject to adversarial procedures that often delay or limit them. However, the other benefits can be invaluable to victims who exhaust compensation benefits, choose not to report their crimes, or are ineligible for compensation due to contributory conduct or other factors.

OPTIONS FOR IMPROVING SOCIAL WELFARE AND OTHER GOVERNMENT PROGRAMS

Each of these programs could be improved individually, as all leave many claimants with unmet needs. One alternative to the traditional provision of benefits is to expand the Earned Income Tax Credit (EITC) program to replace all other benefit systems. This idea for a "negative income tax," first proposed by conservative economist Milton Friedman, would minimize fraud, duplication, and administrative costs. EITCs can be prepaid in payroll transactions. However, if it were to serve crime victims, whose loss of income and need for income replacement is always unexpected and often urgent, a system to make advance payments on an emergency basis would need to be made a component of the plan.

Workers' compensation could be substantially improved if it eliminated the adversarial nature of some of its procedures. While there are clearly attempts to defraud the system by workers, employers, and service providers, and there are also new case circumstances which are not yet reflected in workers' compensation case law, there are also many situations that are both typical and deserving of workers' compensation. This is particularly true of crime victims' claims. If these cases were determined in a less adversarial manner, more quickly, and according to simpler rules, workers' compensation agencies could divert more attention, and resources, to detecting fraud, rooting out service providers who consistently abuse the system, and deliberating over new case circumstances that appear to be prototypes of future cases.

However, the best way to improve these benefits might be to coordinate them under a single umbrella agency. Such an umbrella agency could ensure both that claimants obtain all that they are entitled to and that no one receives com-pensation for the same cost more than once. In the absence of such an overarching agency, liaisons should be developed among those benefit providers who work together most frequently (such as staffs of crime victim compensation and workers' compensation programs) and benefits that often go to victims, such as witness fees, should be provided through crime victim compensation agencies.

SUMMARY

There is a large array of benefits for which crime victims may become eligible, many of which are not based on victim status. It is important that these benefits be assessed not only individually, but jointly, to ensure that crime victims can have the bulk of their needs met by them in some combination.

NOTES

1. These benefit summaries are primarily based on explanations of the benefits found in Gertrude Schaffner Goldberg, *Government Money For Everyday People* (New York: Ginn Press for Adelphi University, 1991).

2. At 1995 tax rates.

3. Referred to by different names in some states, such as Medi-Cal in California.

5

Civil Litigation

Originally there was no distinction between criminal and civil law. But as the criminal justice system evolved, it became necessary to distinguish between areas of the law that fell within the criminal domain (i.e., crimes against the state) and those that remained in the civil, or "tort" arena (Epstein 1977).

In medieval times "composition," as reimbursement was then called, was determined by agreement of the parties involved, with governments intervening only when disputes could not be settled, as in our current civil practice (Epstein 1977). Gradually, however, governments began to charge fees for intervening in increasingly contested reimbursement cases. Then, during the twelfth century, as the central power in the community increased, the community's share of compensation also increased, until finally the king or overlord took the entire payment (Schafer 1977).

During the process of change from individual action to central authority, the interests of the state gradually overshadowed and supplanted those of the victim. The connection between reimbursement and punishment was severed. Victim rights and the concepts of composition and restitution were separated from the criminal law and became incorporated into the civil law of torts (Schafer 1970).

In the Anglo-American legal system, there is now a strict separation of criminal law from civil law. Instead of a separate civil proceeding, in many countries, including Germany, criminal cases and civil actions are combined (Schafer 1970). Even in these countries, however, victims seldom receive full compensation for the harm done to them by criminals. After making a comparative survey of the methods for providing restitution to victims now in effect in various countries of the world, Stephen Schafer (1970) stated that, "if one looks at the legal systems of different countries, one seeks in vain a country where a victim enjoys a certain expectation of full [reimbursement] for his injury."

THE STATE OF THE ART OF CIVIL LITIGATION AS A MEANS OF REIMBURSING CRIME VICTIMS

Crime victims may initiate civil lawsuits against their assailants or anyone else (including corporate entities, and in limited cases, governmental ones) who can be held responsible for a crime's occurrence. Landlords, private security firms, schools, and businesses have been successfully sued for failing to take adequate precautions to protect people using their services, and payments in some such cases have been quite high.

However, not all crimes lend themselves to these types of lawsuits, and victims' needs have no relation to the potential for civil payments. Such cases also take years to litigate and take severe emotional tolls on victims (Barbieri 1989). Most important, these cases require "deep pockets" if the settlements that result are to be anything but nominal. This usually limits civil litigation to lawsuits against people and organizations that are rich or well-insured. It has been made more difficult by recent attempts at tort reform and court decisions that, while they have varied, have more frequently determined that automobile and homeowners' insurance policies do not cover intentional acts such as child molestation (Cleary 1989, Grady 1989).

Pain and suffering is primarily compensated in the civil arena. This has the advantage that claims are determined individually, and far more liberally, than if awards were made statutorily uniform, as they would be if paid by a state compensation program (Spence 1989). However, the result is that very few victims receive awards for pain and suffering (Stark and Goldstein 1985).

It should be noted, too, that in some jurisdictions victims may receive pain and suffering payments through restitution provisions. It is the deep pockets, and not the mechanism for reimbursement, that makes civil litigation likelier to result in pain and suffering payments than restitution. Deep pockets suggest more generous payments, as well.

CIVIL LITIGATION AGAINST OFFENDERS

Whether or not an offender has been found guilty in a criminal proceeding, that offender can be sued civilly by his or her victims or their survivors (Stark and Goldstein 1985). With the increased interest in victims' rights, additional attention is being paid to civil litigation against offenders as a means for victims to collect all that is due to them, and perhaps to exact additional revenge against criminals, as well. However, rules that limit insurance payments to negligent acts frequently close off insurance to victims who were intentionally harmed by their attackers.

Another potential source of funds for at least some civil litigation actions appears to be even more controversial. Thomas Jacobson, attorney for eight of the eleven families of Jeffrey Dahmer's victims, attempted to have Dahmer's possessions sold at auction for the families' benefit (Siemaszko 1996). Jacobson —and the families—were criticized for this, and no auction house would handle the "murderabilia" (Kuntzman 1996). Finally, a Milwaukee civic group raised a half million dollars to "buy" the families out of the auction. However, they did so out of concern for their city's image rather than the families' needs ("Auction to Sell" 1996). It is ironic that, while manufacturers have profited from the sale of materials related to sensational criminals (collectors' cards of serial murderers being only one example), there appears to be opposition to victims obtaining funds in this way.

Victims often feel that they have more rights in the civil arena, where they can hire their own attorneys rather than relying on the state to prosecute its case, in which victims are witnesses at best. Rules of evidence also give the victim a greater chance of proving that the defendant was at fault, even if the evidence was inadequate to sustain a guilty verdict in criminal court (Office for Victims of Crime 1993). Defendants are unable to invoke the Fifth Amendment in civil matters, and cannot avoid liability by claiming insanity. And a jury can determine guilt by a majority, there is no need for a unanimous verdict in civil cases, while a lesser standard of proof, "preponderance of evidence," makes it easier for a civil jury to determine guilt than in a criminal trial, when "beyond a reasonable doubt" is the standard. The family of Ronald Goldman gave such reasons for civilly suing O. J. Simpson for Goldman's death (McCombs 1995).

Therefore, it is important that the effectiveness of civil litigation against offenders be objectively evaluated. Unlike other forms of reimbursement, most people, and even most victims, know only what the media informs them about civil litigation. However, several important questions about these cases must be answered if they are to be considered serious alternatives to compensation. These questions include:

- What proportion of these suits succeed, what proportion fail, and how many victims drop their cases rather than see them through to settlement? How long does the average case take to litigate, and what are the parameters of case length?
- What are the offender—and victim—characteristics that make these kinds of cases successful and unsuccessful?
- What are the factors likely to make a civil case against a criminal emotionally damaging to the victim, and how can they be determined in advance?
- How willing and able are attorneys to take these cases?
- Do all victims have access to attorneys who will at least assess the merits of their cases?
- Should compensation programs hire attorneys to advise victims about civil litigation and file lawsuits on behalf of those who wish to pursue them?
- How many suits are actually brought? How many are settled out of court? How many are won in trial? How many are successfully appealed?
- What are the actual proceeds of these cases after appeal?

Civil lawsuits merit attention in particular cases in which victims might not be eligible for other compensation, or offenders might have a greater than usual ability to pay damages. These cases are especially important when they can right egregious wrongs that compensation agencies were not designed to address, and when they alert the public to specific dangers. Corporate crime and professional malpractice, in particular, fit these conditions (Mokhiber 1988, Besharov and Besharov 1987). As the public becomes more aware of the extent of corporate and "white-collar" crimes, the seriousness of the damages they cause to health and safety, and the leniency of existing criminal laws against such conduct, it can be expected that civil lawsuits against violently criminal corporations will increase in use and effectiveness.

THIRD-PARTY CIVIL LITIGATION

Third-party civil litigation is not unlike civil litigation against the offender. It is often characterized as a search for "deeper pockets" when it is obvious that the offender is financially unable to pay on a claim otherwise owed.

Third-party litigation was never meant to be simply a search for someone with the resources to reimburse a victim, however—the law specifically enumerates circumstances under which individuals' negligence can be considered "contributory" to a criminal act (Carrington and Rapp 1989). Nonetheless, personal injury attorneys have stretched these definitions so that today "negligence" is often overlooked by juries in an effort "not to redress individual victims for acts of irresponsibility, but to redistribute goods more equitably" (Herrnstein and Murray 1994). This is particularly true when an individual sues a business or governmental entity which is presumed to carry extensive insurance coverage (deFrancis et al. 1995). And most third-party involvement in crime is negligent rather than intentional, as when a landlord is sued for a faulty lock that allowed a criminal access to an apartment, or an employer is sued for failing to conduct an adequate background check on an employee who later injures a coworker.

Governmental bodies generally have immunity in such cases. However, recent cases have been interpreted very narrowly, so that while governments are not responsible merely because a crime occurred, they can be held responsible if they were specifically guilty of failure to protect, respond, fulfill a duty, warn, act competently, restrain, comply, adequately train and supervise, or rescue in a timely manner (Carrington and Rapp 1989).

For example, several cases have been successfully pressed against police departments that failed to respond or did not respond promptly, by women who were battered despite the fact that they had orders of protection against their assailants. While these cases are still rare, they have been instrumental in encouraging police departments to be more responsive to domestic violence.

Victims have also recently filed lawsuits against the New York City Transit Authority for failing to prevent subway crime (Hoffman 1995), and the New York City Department of Social Services for failing to prevent child abuse in its foster care system (Smith and Schwartzman 1995), and for failing to properly follow up calls to its child abuse hotline (Hernandez 1996). The results of these cases will help to determine the future trend of civil litigation against government entities.

School administrations have particularly significant responsibilities, especially when they act in the place of parents, as well as when they act as landlords (Carrington and Rapp 1989). Similarly, common carriers, employers, innkeepers, and parents have special responsibilities toward people in their charge, and are the most common groups against whom negligence cases are filed (Carrington and Rapp 1989). Medical and mental health practitioners have special liability if they mistreat or fail to consult, refer, or protect patients (Besharov and Besharov 1987).

Third-party lawsuits also have been used against groups that incite violence. Attorney Morris Dees successfully sued the Ku Klux Klan and the White Aryan Resistance for inciting members to kill black people, and the damages appear to have bankrupted both groups (London 1990).

However, a bizarre twist to this type of lawsuit has been developed in the form of the Pornography Victims Compensation Act. The proposed legislation would enable victims of certain, usually sexual, crimes to sue the producers or sellers of pornographic works on the grounds that they "caused" the crimes to be committed. Not only is this bill clearly in opposition to the First Amendment; it has no basis in fact (sex criminals tend to have had *less* exposure to pornography than have others) (Donnerstein, Linz, and Penrod 1987); and it shifts the blame for crime from offenders (Heins 1992).

Other attempts to stretch third-party liability, which emanate from the desire to make manufacturers and employers more responsible, similarly mix contributory negligence and blame-shifting. For example, the wife of an NBC stagehand who was killed by a mentally ill man who believed that NBC was controlling his brain, filed lawsuits against the owners of Rockefeller Center, NBC's security service, the manufacturer of the rifle used in the crime, and the importer of the weapon (VanGelder 1994). Opposition to such lawsuits is contributing to the increasing call for tort reform, which particularly aims to limit lawsuits based on product liability but also seeks caps on all damages (Kuttner 1996). This has the potential to affect every victim of crime who sues civilly.

Due to the small number of third-party civil litigation cases in relation to victimizations, it is important that their effectiveness be objectively evaluated. In addition to the questions asked above, the following issues should be explored if third-party civil litigation is to be considered a serious alternative to compensation:

- What proportion of these suits succeed, what proportion fail, and how many victims drop their cases rather than see them through to settlement? Which types of third parties are successfully sued? Which are the most difficult to sue successfully?
- Which groups are most able and likely to pay judgments against them?
- What is the political impact of prosecuting these cases, particularly when they point up inadequacies on the part of governmental bodies?
- Should compensation programs hire attorneys to advise victims about third-party civil litigation and assist victims to file lawsuits—or file them on behalf of those who wish to pursue them?
- Should compensation program attorneys file suits in "victimless" cases on behalf of society, with awards going to a fund pool for victims who are not compensated by offenders or other sources?

Like civil litigation against offenders, third party civil lawsuits merit attention in particular cases in which the victim might not be eligible for other compensation, the offender may be better able to pay than most, the vigilance of a negligent individual or organization might be improved, or a third-party clearly incited a crime.

NOTORIETY-FOR-PROFIT LEGISLATION

In 1977, a series of random shootings in New York City by an unknown assailant, who contacted the media under the alias "Son of Sam," raised speculation that the killer's story, if he was located, would command a considerable fee. Outraged at the idea that a criminal could profit from a crime in this way, New York State Senator Emmanuel Gold introduced a statute that would hold any such funds in escrow for the victims depicted in the story (Stark and Goldstein 1985). By 1987, 37 states had adopted some form of notoriety-for-profit legislation, and in 1984 a corresponding federal statute was enacted (Hazelip 1987).

Ironically, in 1991 the United States Supreme Court unanimously overturned New York's "Son of Sam" law, finding it in violation of the First Amendment of the United States Constitution. In the Supreme Court justices' decisions, they noted that the statute prohibited expression and that it singled out a particular type of expression for repression ("High Court" 1991). This has forced all states and the federal government to review and revise their notoriety for profit statutes. New York's Senator Gold has since introduced legislation, enacted shortly thereafter, that extends the statute of limitations to enable victims to recover damages from offenders who earn money from their depictions of crimes (or from any other means) long after those crimes occur (Verhovek 1992).

One attempt to use the new law has already identified an important limitation of notoriety-for-profit legislation (which would have been as true of the old law as the new one). Attorney Eric Naiburg argued that his client Amy Fischer's story could be sold to raise her bail (and presumably to enable her to retain counsel) because she was innocent until proven guilty (Goldstein 1992). While this may seem like an exception to notoriety-for-profit legislation, it actually ensures that the law cannot be used to prevent accused people from mounting strong defenses, and may prove a means of enabling victims of false allegations or politically motivated criminal charges to fully exercise their right to a fair trial.

As notoriety-for-profit cases are so rare, they certainly will not supplant compensation. But their value should be assessed by considering other issues, such as:

- How many potential claims of this type exist, and what proportion of victims who are eligible to file such claims do so?
- Is there value in offender's stories, and should this be compromised in the name of victims' rights?
- Do authors have the right to write about private citizens without sharing their profits with those citizens, or compensating them for lost privacy?

- Might unclaimed notoriety-for-profit funds be channeled to fund victim services broadly, especially when there are no specific, identifiable victims of particular crimes?
- What portion of offenders attempt to exploit their notoriety?
- What, if any, harm does such notoriety cause victims?
- What is the effect of the notoriety these cases gain on the victims' movement?
- Is the administration of notoriety-for-profit legislation justified by the income it generates, or by any other factor?

LIMITATIONS OF CIVIL LITIGATION

In theory, Anglo-American crime victims have for centuries had available to them the civil remedy of tort action against persons who have wronged them through the commission of crimes. In practice, however, this remedy has been of little value. Offenders are often unknown, and when they are known, victims often cannot afford the expense, in terms of money and time, to bring tort actions against them (Wolfgang 1965). And, because perpetrators of crimes are typically poor (Geis 1967), judgments against offenders are often uncollectible.

As a result, very few such suits are brought, most often because offenders' lack of assets make them financially impractical (Stark and Goldstein 1985). There is also concern that civil litigation can adversely affect victims' psychological recovery (Barbieri 1989). No one knows, however, how many such suits might be brought if victims were more aware of this remedy.

While civil lawsuits are often costly in time and emotional drain, attorneys take these cases on a contingency basis, charging a fee only if the case is won. This means, however, that attorneys are often unwilling to take on such cases unless the evidence is extremely strong and the offender is able to pay significant damages (Villmoore and Neto 1987). Civil attorneys also make up for possible losses by charging very high fees when they win—usually one-third of the proceeds of the case. As attorney William M. Evarts said of contingency fees, "If I don't win your suit, I get nothing. If I do win it, you get nothing" (Hay 1989).

In fact, in 1986 alone, Americans spent $30 billion on damage lawsuits, but collected only half that amount in settlements, with legal fees and court costs accounting for the remainder (Nishimura 1990). Furthermore, civil litigation is not completely "free"; victims must often pay filing fees and deposition costs out of pocket, before their cases are settled and regardless of whether they are likely to be won (United States Department of Justice 1993). Civil lawsuits take many years to resolve, and often that time is artificially extended by insurance companies in order to make victims more desperate for payments, as interest accrues in the insurer's account, which may be adequate to cover the victim's claim without having to draw on the principle (Spence 1989).

Elias (1983) observed that most civil lawsuits against offenders fail, and that in the few successful ones, the damages awarded are insufficient to cover both restitution and legal fees. It is also common for offenders to declare bankruptcy to avoid paying judgments against them (Lewin 1990, Carrington and Rapp 1989).

Spence (1989) observed that most people are aware of the few large settlements awarded in such cases, but not of the fact that even these are often substantially reduced on appeal. Then, too, if victims win they must reimburse any means-tested government benefits, including crime victim compensation and Medicaid.

Large settlements, if awarded, can bring problems of their own. Victims are often advised not to bring civil proceedings until after a criminal case is completed, because defense attorneys have used the possibility of filing a civil suit as a motive for a victim to lie during criminal proceedings. Furthermore, "blood money" obtained in civil cases, especially when the victim has died, can make survivors feel guilty about profiting from their loved one's misfortune. Spence (1989) suggests using such funds as a "living memorial" to the victim, by donating them to charity or setting up a scholarship fund, to avoid this result.

Proponents of notoriety-for-profit legislation are understandably outraged that imprisoned authors can once again earn money telling the stories of their crimes. Some even suggest that expanding the law to cover journalists would help victims regain privacy. In fact, New Jersey attempted to use its Son of Sam law to lien the profits that author Flora Rheta Schreiber made on her book, *The Shoemaker*, about serial killer Joseph Kallinger. However, New Jersey courts recognized this to be unfair restraint, because Dr. Schreiber had committed no crime.

Those who lament the loss of the "Son of Sam" law should note that in New York State, during the law's fourteen-year tenure, only $71,450 was recovered by victims as a result of its existence (Hevesi 1991). Furthermore, New York, the hub of publishing in the United States, was one of only two states that saw *any* economic gain from this type of legislation; notoriety-for-profit legislation accounted for less than .1 percent of compensation revenues nationwide (Parent, Auerbach, and Carlson 1992).

Opponents of the laws cite not only constitutional questions, but value-based ones, as well. Is there some utility in reading an offender's story, if only to better understand criminals and the motivation for committing crimes? Proponents counter that offenders can still write their stories, only their right to profit from them is compromised by the law. But that loss of profit is a serious deterrent, as was proven when Hedda Nussbaum chose not to sell her story to a television network after New York State attempted to place a lien on her profits from it.

No one can say how many offenders have opted not to tell their stories only because they would have lost the revenues that those stories would have brought them as a result of notoriety-for-profit legislation. But the effect of these laws suggests that some proponents may have as their aim more than victim reimbursement—they may simply want to silence offenders.

There is considerable evidence, for example, that suppression of offenders' writing is most often used against political prisoners. If such legislation had existed in the past, in fact, it might have suppressed works by the Berrigan brothers, Dorothy Day, Eugene Debs, Marcus Garvey, Emma Goldman, Dick Gregory, Joe Hill, Mother Jones, Martin Luther King, Margaret Sanger, and Henry David Thoreau, as well as by nonpolitical prisoners Jack Henry Abbot, Claude Brown, William S. Burroughs, Eldridge Cleaver, John Erlichmann, Ralph

Ginzburg, Merle Haggard, H. R. Haldemann, Jean Harris, Billie Holiday, E. Howard Hunt, George Jackson, G. Gordon Liddy, Jeb Stuart Magruder, Ethel and Julius Rosenberg, Nicola Sacco, Bartolomeo Vanzetti and Malcolm X (Franklin 1989).

Finally, the process of civil litigation is so time-consuming that it cannot meet the needs of crime victims in a timely way. However, it can serve to reimburse victims more fully, provided they have other sources of funds to meet their needs, and can reimburse those sources from civil litigation proceeds when they become available.

OPTIONS FOR IMPROVING CIVIL LITIGATION

Mueller and Cooper (1975) recommend recombining the civil and criminal proceedings to save the victim the burden of going through two separate trials for the same crime. As noted, this is done in many European countries, and is the historical model, as well. Such a proceeding could integrate the assessment of victims' needs with offenders' ability to pay, as has been recommended when assessing restitution. Making the criminal justice system less adversarial, and linking it to reimbursement, could lead to a re-melding of civil and criminal procedures, so victims would not have to go to court a second time to obtain civil damages. However, for such a melding process to occur, it would first be necessary to determine how to deal with two separate degrees of proof or whether it would be possible to create a single one without eroding some offenders' or victims' rights in the process.

It is also important that civil litigation not be used to discriminate against poor criminals while keeping higher-income-producing criminals out of prison. In fact, there needs to be more recognition of the fact that white-collar crime can be extremely violent, and even homicidal, as class-action lawsuits against manufacturers of breast implants, intrauterine devices, and cigarettes, and perpetrators of environmental spills have legally established (Mokhiber 1988). Furthermore, by making the public more aware of the danger of white collar crime it may be possible to reduce racism, because Americans fear street crime (Jencks 1992), which is disproportionately committed by members of minority groups, more than crimes of the equally violent white collar variety, which are less often committed by minorities if only because they have less access to white collar jobs.

Another alternative, used in at least one Iowa case ("Jury Awards" 1992), granted 25 percent of a $4.3 million settlement to the victims, and the remainder to the Iowa State Reparations Fund. In this case, the victims clearly received an award for pain and suffering, and the satisfaction of seeing the offender heavily penalized. However, some of this heavy penalty was distributed to other needy victims, rather than allowing the victims to profit unduly. This is also a way of separating compensatory damages, paid to victims for their costs and suffering, from punitive damages assessed against offenders as a punishment, which do not necessarily have to be paid to the victim. More accurately, this type of financial split reimburses both the *direct* victim of crime and society, as a less direct, but similarly victimized, entity.

Victim compensation programs could increase their subrogation potential by screening compensation claims for factors that would make civil litigation particularly likely to result in payments to victims, and by helping them to access these payments. This might include revising notoriety-for-profit and other civil litigation legislation to permit uncollected funds to go to a general fund for victims, as in the Iowa case. In particular, as noted, separate determinations could be made for compensatory damages, payable only to victims or their survivors, and punitive damages, which could be distributed to victims more broadly or earmarked for educational or preventive purposes.

Victim compensation programs might also consider filing class-action lawsuits against offending corporations on behalf of all state residents, to expand their purviews to additional victims of crime. This would be likely to have a deterrent effect on such crimes, as well as more effectively offset the costs of crime.

However, victim compensation agencies must not design their programs to supplant civil remedies, as workers' compensation does toward employers, because that would only limit victims' reimbursement options. Instead, they should focus on providing timely, basic compensation to meet victims' needs while victims investigate other avenues of reimbursement. It is also important to facilitate civil litigation and restitution whenever possible, because experts agree that victims prefer reimbursement to be paid directly by their assailants (Antilla 1986, Shapland 1986, Carrow 1980).

At one time, workers' compensation precluded workers from any further action against their employers (Skocpol 1992). Today, more and more civil lawsuits are being pressed—and won—against employers, particularly if the employers were aware of a hazard or were extremely negligent about safety. Victims of workplace violence have also had success in suing negligent security and background-checking firms and even coworkers. As one expert noted,

workplace . . . crimes are increasingly being viewed by the legal system, the government and employers themselves as occupational health threats that are potentially preventable, rather than simply as random acts by criminals. . . . Survivors of murdered employees have won sizable sums in civil suits against employers or others with responsibilities in workplaces. (Purdy 1994)

It seems, however, that the only advantage of civil litigation is that its threat may impel some employers to improve the safety of their workplaces. Concern for their reputations, consumer demand, and regulatory agencies probably have a greater impact on more employers than do liability concerns. It must be noted, however, that "Legal rules and policy *will* be made, in courts if not by legislatures, with or without data" [italics in original] (Huber and Litan 1991). Therefore, civil litigation will continue to be a means of proving liability for violence, until it is addressed more effectively by legislators, government agencies, insurers and the general public.

SUMMARY

Civil litigation can result in pain and suffering payments to victims, which only two state compensation programs and rare restitution orders cover. However, civil litigation requires that the defendant have sufficient funds to reimburse the victim. If a third party is the defendant, negligence on that person's part must also be proven.

Finally, notoriety-for-profit laws are being rewritten to resemble civil litigation legislation with extended statutes of limitation. While all of these offer significant coverage to those victims whose circumstances match their intricate requirements, they fail to help many needy victims whose crime circumstances do not happen to fit these criteria.

6

Crime Victim Compensation

In 1968, the federal government developed the Law Enforcement Assistance Administration (LEAA). LEAA was created to provide funds for research and demonstration projects to identify the needs of victims as well as to develop innovative ways to meet those needs. LEAA became defunct in 1981, on the grounds that by then the states, aware of the needs of victims and better able to address them, would also be able and willing to fund them.

By the early 1980s, most states had developed victim services of some type. However, programs varied in size and scope as well as in the populations they served. The most common services were rape crisis programs. While most rape crisis programs were poorly funded, they managed to remain in operation after the loss of LEAA funds because they had always relied on volunteers to provide the bulk of their services. Many domestic violence shelters had also been created with LEAA funds, but they could not fall back on volunteers alone, because the services they provide, such as housing, food, medical care, and child care, are far more cost-intensive (Schechter 1984).

As a result, many domestic violence services were lost, and many geographic areas remained unserved by any type of victim service programs. Even victims who received help from these services were left with unmet needs, because few of the programs had resources to meet all of the needs of all kinds of victims. Finally, services varied widely from place to place, so victims could not expect to receive similar services or levels of service even in different parts of the same state.

To remedy this, the federal government developed a new source of funds for victim compensation and other victim services, from pooled federal fines against criminals. In 1982, the Victims of Crime Act (VOCA) was created to encourage states to develop compensation programs and to set minimum standards for VOCA fund recipients, by offering matching funds to state crime victim compensation programs that complied with VOCA guidelines (United States Department of

Justice 1982). The standards were updated in 1989, and VOCA funds were made permanent in 1991. In 1996, VOCA added the requirement that by 1998, states must cover their residents for acts of terrorism which occur in foreign countries (*Crime Victim Compensation Quarterly* 1996).

THE STATE OF THE ART OF CRIME VICTIM COMPENSATION

As a result, all fifty states have developed some form of compensation to crime victims. Forty-eight of them qualified for VOCA funds in 1995, and Maine's program qualified in 1996. Only Nevada chooses not to participate in VOCA, although that state does operate a victim compensation program (United States Department of Justice, undated).

In 1989, VOCA revised its guidelines to require its recipients to compensate victims of drunk drivers and domestic violence, and to require coverage for lost wages and medical, mental health, and funeral costs. More specifically, VOCA-funded states are now prohibited from denying compensation to entire categories of victims, such as victims of domestic violence, or for broad reasons such as the mere fact that a victim is related to or living with the offender. States can set guidelines to prevent unjust enrichment of the offender, but they must develop clear criteria for making this determination (Parent, Auerbach, and Carlson 1992).

Prior to 1984, 35 states had developed crime victim compensation programs of some type. Each was designed independently, so the programs bore only vague similarities to each other. The provision of VOCA funds in 1984, which were made available to those programs that adhered to the newly created federal guidelines, brought the programs into somewhat greater uniformity. Compensation programs still appear to be more dissimilar than similar, however, and their eligibility criteria and benefit levels not only differ greatly but change over time. This is true in part because of the diversity among the states—in size, population, geography, and resources, as well as in their political and philosophical differences (Carrow 1980).

It is also important to understand that victims are usually eligible for crime victim compensation benefits only in the state where the crime occurred. A few states offer benefits to both residents and people victimized there (with no safeguards against "double dipping"). In addition, because Nevada does not participate in VOCA, victims of federal crimes in Nevada can apply to any other state compensation program for reimbursement.

Smith and Freinkel (1988) noted that the earliest victim compensation programs began in the 1960s, as social programs in general were being created or expanded. Like other social programs of the period, crime victim compensation programs started at this time were created to quell social unrest among the poor. Therefore, they tended to be targeted to the poor with means tests, but most have expanded their services and dropped or liberalized their means tests since then.

From 1974 through 1983, an additional 27 programs were added. The reasons for their creation differed from those of the programs started in the 1960s and early 1970s. These new programs were primarily "law-and-order" oriented, having been started as a backlash to a perceived increase in "offenders' rights."[1] Exceptions were a handful of programs started in response to single cases or single-issue advocacy, which reflected such priorities in their guidelines (Smith and Freinkel 1988).

Finally, the remaining programs were clearly started primarily as a response to the availability of federal VOCA matching funds. In fact, Rhode Island enacted enabling legislation in 1976, but its victim compensation program did not become operational until federal funds became available in 1984 (Carrow 1980).

The most critical policy options available to compensation programs are coverage, eligibility criteria, and benefits. Coverage refers to both the types of losses and the types of crimes compensated. VOCA requires programs to cover medical, mental health, and funeral expenses as well as lost wages. Thirty-seven victim compensation programs also covered rehabilitation services and 35 included replacement services. Moving costs, property replacement, and pain and suffering were covered by only a few programs (Parent, Auerbach, and Carlson 1992).

Some victim compensation programs contained their costs by the use of caps, fee schedules, and other mechanisms. Fee schedules determine maximum amounts that will be paid for specific medical procedures. Caps, on the other hand, determine the total amount that can be paid in a cost category. In general, fee schedules place the responsibility for cost containment on service providers, while caps limit services to victims (although they may also protect victims from excessive or unnecessary treatment). Caps on the most commonly covered costs are shown in Table 6.1, which demonstrates that 15 states capped their total benefits at $10,000 and 13 capped them at $25,000, with the range spanning from $5,000 in Georgia, Maine, and New Hampshire to New York's uncapped maximum.

Medical costs make up the bulk of victim compensation payments in almost all victim compensation programs. This is not surprising, because medical costs have been increasing everywhere, but are highest in the United States, where administration, advertising, and profit account for between 19 percent and 24 percent of total medical costs (Woolhandler and Himmelstein 1991).

Some victim compensation programs have followed the lead of private insurers by adopting fee schedules capping the allowable costs they will pay for procedures. Fee capping can have different results depending on how it is structured. If caps are low, some providers will refuse to accept them as full payment. They will either charge victims the difference between their fees and the cap, or, if this is not permitted, refuse to treat crime victims who must rely on compensation to pay their medical bills. If caps are reasonable, or if the number of patients whose treatment is covered by compensation is large, providers will be more inclined to serve victims eligible for compensation benefits.

While not all programs use them, fee schedules appear to be the primary method of cost-containment used by victim compensation programs. In addition, most programs reserve the right to send claimants to agency-paid providers for second opinions, to ensure that the treatment they receive is necessary and appropriate.

Table 6.1
Caps on Compensation Benefits by Type
(ranked by maximum benefit)

STATE	MAXIMUM BENEFIT	MEDICAL	MENTAL HEALTH	FUNERAL	WAGES/ SUPPORT	ATTORNEY FEES	EMERGENCY AWARDS
New York	no limit			$2000	$20000	$1000	$1500
Washington	$150,000			$1100	$40000		$1500
Minnesota	$50,000		$75/session	$3700			
Ohio	$50,000			$2500			
California	$46,000		50 session	$3500		10%	$1000
Maryland	$45,000		$2000	$2000	$25000	$50/hour	$1000
Wisconsin	$40,000			$2000		10%	$500
Alaska	$40,000						
Pennsylvania	$35,000			$3750	$20000	15%	$1000
Connecticut	$25,000			$2500		15%	$1000
Delaware	$25,000	$5000	$5000	$4500		15%	$1000
Idaho	$25,000	$2500	$2500	$2500	$175/week	5%	$1000
Illinois	$25,000			$3000	$1000/month		
Kansas	$25,000		$3500	$2000	$200/week	$225	
Kentucky	$25,000			$3500	$150/week	15%	$500
Massachusetts	$25,000			$2000		15%	
Montana	$25,000			$2000		5%	
New Jersey	$25,000		50 sessions	$3000	$300/week	15%	$1500
N Dakota	$25,000			$1500		$2000	
Rhode Island	$25,000						
Texas	$25,000		$3000	$3000	$200/week		$1500
Utah	$25,000		$2500	$3500			$1000
Oregon	$23,000	$10000	$10000	$2000			$1000
N Carolina	$22,000	$20000	$20000	$2000	$5200		$5000

State							
Iowa	$20,600	$10600	$3000	$5000	$6000		$500
W Virginia	$20,000			$3000			$3500
New Mexico	$20,000			$3000		15%	$500
Michigan	$15,000			$1500	$200/week		$1000
Nevada	$15,000			$1000	$200/week		$2000
Virginia	$15,000			$2000	$200/week		
Alabama	$10,000		$3500	$3000	$200/week		$500
Arizona	$10,000		12 months	$1500	$130/week		$500
Arkansas	$10,000		$2500	$2500	$200/week		$500
Colorado	$10,000		$1000	varies			$500
Florida	$10,000		$2500	$2000	$425/week	15%	$500
Hawaii	$10,000	$2500	$3000	$3000		15%	$500
Indiana	$10,000	$3000	$1000	$3000		$250	
Louisiana	$10,000		$2000	$2000	$5200	15%	$500
Mississippi	$10,000		$1000	$1000	$3000	$500	$500
Missouri	$10,000		$1000	$2000	$200/week	$500	$500
Nebraska	$10,000		$2000	$3000	$265/week		
Oklahoma	$10,000			$2500	$200/week	10%	$500
S Carolina	$10,000		15 sessions	$2000			
S Dakota	$10,000			$4500	$500/week		$500
Wyoming	$10,000			$3000	$1500/month		
Vermont	$10,000		$3000	$4500		15%	$1000
Tennessee	$7,000		$2500	$3000			
Maine	$5,000				$200/week		$500
New Hampshire	$5,000		$2000	$2000			
Georgia	$5,000		$2500	$2500			$1000

Note: Data obtained from National Association of Crime Victim Compensation Boards (1993, 1994) and Parent, Auerbach, and Carlson (1992).

Another factor that affects total medical costs is their scope of coverage. For example, rehabilitation and long-term care are not covered by most public and private benefits, but are paid by some victim compensation programs. In addition, medical supplies, such as prescription medicines, even if they were stolen during a robbery and are not used to treat crime-caused injuries, and medical devices, such as glasses and walkers, are sometimes covered under this category.

Mental health costs are the costs that are rising most precipitously for victim compensation programs. Although they made up fewer than 2 percent of all compensation program costs in 1986, they had risen to 48 percent of program costs by 1991 (National Association of Crime Victim Compensation Boards 1994b). Twenty-eight victim compensation programs separately capped mental health costs, with California, New Jersey, and South Carolina limiting only the number of sessions, Minnesota's capping only the per-session fee, Arizona limiting only the time counseling can continue, and the remaining 15 capping total dollars paid for mental health counseling.

New Jersey set maximum sessions for chiropractic and physical therapy treatment and used a fee schedule for mental health counseling (New Jersey Violent Crimes Compensation Board 1990), while New York used that state's workers' compensation fee schedule for all medical procedures (New York State Crime Victims Board 1990). New Mexico developed a fee policy for Native American Medicine Man treatment, demonstrating not only cultural sensitivity but that it is possible to set fee guidelines for any type of service when basic service criteria are known (New Mexico Crime Victim Reparation Commission 1991).

Alabama took a different approach by developing a Peer Review Panel to review mental health claims and treatment plans (Alabama Crime Victims Compensation Commission 1991). This offered the added benefit of qualitatively as well as quantitatively assessing mental health services. Kansas's mental health policy also ensured quality service by limiting payment to licensed professionals, and informing victims of their rights and responsibilities in the transaction (Kansas Crime Victims Compensation Board, undated).

Mental health counseling is sometimes considered a medical expense, and sometimes calculated separately. Claims for mental health counseling present complex problems, such as whether pre-existing conditions necessitated counseling prior to the victimization. In addition, victim compensation programs are struggling with determining which diagnoses signify "causally related" mental health problems, which types and amounts of treatment are appropriate to the various types of victimization, and what qualifications should be required of those who treat victims (United States Department of Justice 1990).

Funeral costs present a number of unusual circumstances for policy makers. The urgent nature of these payments necessitates a hurried consideration of the facts of these cases. Yet homicides are the most difficult crimes to investigate because the deceased victim is unable to offer verbal evidence. In addition, such contributory conduct as prostitution or the purchase of drugs hardly warrant a death sentence, making the evaluation of victim conduct particularly problematic. Finally, the "victims" of homicide served by victim compensation programs are actually "secondary victims," who are often completely innocent even when indiscretions on the parts of their loved ones may have contributed to the crimes against them. Victim compensation programs also vary in whether they cap funeral costs, although the states that do not cap them tend to have low overall caps. Most programs cap funeral costs, with caps ranging from $1,000 to $5,000, as Table 6.1 demonstrates. Colorado is unusual in that its funeral caps are set locally rather than statewide.

Lost wages are compensation for money that would have been earned from work if the victim had been able to work instead of being treated for or recuperating from injuries resulting from the crime or attending to criminal justice functions. Lost wages do not cover court appearances, however, because these funds are available through district attorneys' offices as witness fees, even though witness fees are rarely paid, as noted in Chapter 4. Victim compensation programs generally require proof of past earnings in the form of pay stubs or income tax records. This precludes people who work in illegal occupations, or who fail to report their incomes for tax purposes, from obtaining wage compensation.

Lost support is compensation for money that the victim had routinely contributed to the support of someone else, which is no longer available because the victim has died. Replacement costs are compensation for necessary services that were supplied without payment by a victim who is no longer able to perform them due to injury or death.

Wages are fairly easy to calculate and verify. Often, wages are covered by other benefits, such as public or private disability insurance. Wages are generally verified by tax returns, and victims can be reimbursed only for those wages which they legally earned and reported to the IRS.

Lost support is often more difficult to calculate, unless there is a separation agreement or divorce decree outlining specified payments to be made by the victim. Often, people support others without such formal agreements. This may include supporting elderly parents, children born out of wedlock, or unmarried partners.

Some victim compensation programs specify who may receive lost support, often ruling out unmarried partners and even estranged spouses. Some also limit support to those who receive *substantial* or even *principle* support from a victim. This seeks to eliminate claims by parents or others to whom a victim was paying "room and board" to cover such items as meals and telephone bills, which do not continue after the death of the victim, as well as claims from roommates and others who shared expenses but did not contribute to each others' needs.

Table 6.1 includes the wage caps for those programs that cap wages. Most cap weekly wages; most of the programs that separately cap wages have high overall caps.

Replacement costs generally refer to the costs of replacing child care and housekeeping services when a parent or spouse is killed or injured so seriously that he or (usually) she is unable to perform these functions. Replacement costs are problematic because there is such a range in the quality and costs of these fee-paid services. Most compensation programs set caps on these services, but there are no data on how they were set or whether the amounts available are sufficient to meet these needs for victims.

Attorneys' fees are covered by some victim compensation programs, while others only allow attorneys' fees to be paid out of victims' awards. When attorneys' fees are paid out of claims, they are paid only on approved claims. This hardly ensures that victims will be able to access compensation (the presumed reason for making attorneys' fees available), because attorneys uncertain of receiving payment may avoid handling victim compensation cases.

On the other hand, a 1975 study by the New York State Legislative Commission on Expenditure Review, which audits the New York State Crime Victims Board, found that claims handled by attorneys resulted in lower payments to victims and took longer to process than claims handled by victims themselves. This difference probably reflects a qualitative difference in claims, however, with attorneys usually handling more complex cases (which may also have a civil component). Since compensation claims are not adversarial in any state, and unless attorney fees can be justified, it might be logical to reserve legal services for appeals, especially in this era of service reductions (Parent, Auerbach, and Carlson 1992).

Table 6.1 shows that 23 programs cap attorneys' fees, although how they do so differs greatly. Six set dollar amounts for the caps, 16 limit caps to a proportion of the total award, and Maryland's victim compensation program caps the hourly fee attorneys can charge claimants. Utah limits attorneys' fees to appeals and assisting minors to establish trusts or guardianships (National Association of Crime Victim Compensation Boards 1993).

Transportation is offered by most victim compensation programs to enable victims to attend to criminal justice matters and to obtain medical treatment. This recognizes the fact that, especially for poor victims, lack of transportation alone may preclude cooperating with authorities, and even seeking needed medical help.

Compensation for non physical injuries is less common. Only four programs compensate pain and suffering, although all compensate for counseling expenses (Stark and Goldstein 1985). As noted, this suggests that counseling can "undo" pain and suffering, although this is not uniformly so either theoretically or in actuality. Nonviolent and motor vehicle crimes are not generally covered except, as VOCA requires, when the driver commits a felony (such as reckless driving or leaving the scene), intentionally inflicts injury, or is intoxicated (Parent, Auerbach, and Carlson 1992).

Property loss is compensated in only limited ways. For example, New York's program covers only $100 of what it terms *essential* personal property (such as home security devices, cash, basic furnishings, and clothing).[2] This is pitifully little compensation considering that it encompasses security devices (such as locks, windows, and doors), as well as cash, food, and other necessities. Iowa covers up to $100 for replacement of clothing held in evidence (Iowa Department of Justice, undated), while Pennsylvania covers lost public benefits (Pennsylvania Crime Victims' Compensation Board 1992). These isolated, and very limited, examples suggest that some programs recognize these special needs of victims, but that property losses due to crime have not been sufficiently addressed, even conceptually, by most victim compensation programs.

Eligibility criteria generally include victims of physical injury, Good Samaritans, and dependents of homicide victims. Victims are excluded if they fail to report the crime to the police, and often if they contribute to their own injuries. Controversially, victims are also excluded if there is a chance that the offender will benefit from the award, as is often the case with battered women who continue to live with their assailants after they had been assaulted.

In 1994, concern that battered women and rape victims who failed to report their crimes to the police were not being adequately served resulted in the creation of the federal Violence Against Women Act (VAWA). VAWA distributed $26 million to the states to improve the criminal justice response to women. A minimum of 25 percent (and a maximum of 50 percent) is allocated to victims' services under VAWA. In addition, the Department of Health and Human Services annually provides funds for rape services and battered women's shelters under their reproductive health and emergency housing divisions, respectively, and state crime victim compensation programs fund programs targeted to these groups. None of these services requires that victims report the crimes against them to the criminal justice system to obtain services (United States Department of Justice 1990).

In fact, it appears that the majority of victim service programs are directed toward these two groups specifically, sometimes individually and sometimes as a single entity (funds targeted to violence against women). This suggests that they are better served than first appearances would indicate. The reality is even less equitable, however. As shelter services are very cost-intensive, and the victims they serve are often ineligible for many benefits, domestic violence services continue to struggle for subsistence. On the other hand, rape crisis services have flourished, although most of these programs have devolved from multi-service centers that sought to raise the consciousness of society to the prevalence and seriousness of rape by helping victims and changing laws and social attitudes, to counseling centers that reinforce victim powerlessness while purporting to restore victims' power and control (Schechter 1984). Currently, nearly 50 percent of recent sexual assault victims, and 9 percent of victims of earlier sexual assaults, receive mental health counseling. Only secondary victims of homicide approach these rates of mental health treatment (Miller, Cohen, and Wiersema 1996).

Ironically, definitions of victimization are also being expanded, often by therapists, so that nearly anyone can be considered to have been abused according to *some* definitions (McElroy 1994, Tavris 1993). Furthermore, those most intent on expanding definitions of abuse also seem to make no differentiation regarding its extent, and tend to assert that all victims require long-term counseling to undo the damage they assume all victims have sustained.

Victim compensation agencies must be careful in these cases to ensure that practitioners do not "create" allegations inappropriately—because practitioners may not be qualified to recognize abuse, or may be unwilling to believe that abuse did *not* occur. Moreover, benefits have the potential to be exploited as a wellspring of third-party payments by any victims willing to claim, or to be convinced by therapists, that they were victimized. Dick Armey has noted that "The key to spending is *always* to make sure that the clients don't get the bill for the service" (Kelly 1992).

While victimization is certainly more widespread than was once imagined, this universalization trivializes the problem—but makes nearly anyone eligible for counseling. This poses several problems for benefit programs, potentially draining resources that are needed to meet other victim needs.

Victim compensation agencies need to develop clear guidelines regarding when adult victims are eligible for counseling based on victimizations that they claim occurred long ago, particularly when those cases are "recalled" after extensive "therapy."[3] This difficult area needs far more attention than it has received to date because, just as it is vital that victims receive adequate, competent treatment, it is also vital to protect clients from overzealous or unqualified mental health practitioners who incorrectly "diagnose" abuse. This issue also needs attention because mental health counseling claims, particularly those based on recent and long-past child sexual abuse, are, as noted, increasing much faster than other types of claims.

While sex crimes must be taken seriously, it is important that they not be equated with ruination, because that only reinforces the objectification of victims, increasing the stigma of sexual assault. One way that this is exemplified is in the fact that 49 percent of recent sexual assault victims receive mental health counseling services, but only 9 percent of past sexual assault victims and only 1-4 percent of victims of crimes other than homicide obtain counseling (Miller, Cohen, and Wiersema 1996). This may suggest particularly zealous outreach to recent victims of sexual assault, or may merely reflect the proliferation of sexual assault programs that have been created since various government entities began to fund them. But it may also suggest overzealous outreach, or the assumption on the part of service providers that victims of sexual assault are particularly in need of mental health services. Is it likely, for example, that victims who are permanently disfigured, or injured to the extent that they cannot resume their livelihoods or their lifestyles (who clearly number above 4 percent of victims of crimes other than sexual assault and homicide), require counseling less frequently than do sexual assault victims?

This suggests that victims choose counseling at far lower rates than sexual assault outreach programs recruit victims. Further evidence that sexual assault is not the most devastating form of victimization is reflected in a study by Widom (1992), which demonstrates that child victims of sexual assault have fewer negative outcomes than child victims of physical abuse or neglect.

Furthermore, some victims might prefer to spend allocations earmarked for counseling in other ways. As noted, compensation programs offer counseling expenses ostensibly to "treat" pain and suffering. But many victims' primary fear after victimization is revictimization. Victims might prefer to take self defense courses, or buy security systems or personal transportation if offered cash in lieu of counseling-specific benefits. It can not be stated that this would be preferable, or more effective, however, because it has never been tried.

Dependents of eligible victims are sometimes eligible for counseling, lost support, or employment training. Victim compensation programs vary in how they define "dependent." In some cases only relatives are eligible, while in others any individuals who were dependent on the victim for the bulk of their support can receive compensation. This difference is critical to unmarried couples, and therefore particularly discriminatory against gay and lesbian couples who cannot legally marry.

Some programs use minimum loss criteria, deductibles, or financial means tests to contain their costs. Time limits on filing further contain costs, and ensure that evidence is still fresh when investigated (Carrow 1980). Yet very brief time limits seem to be an easy way to exclude large numbers of otherwise eligible victims.

All victim compensation programs have some means of excluding victims who contribute to their injuries by their behavior. However, many programs determine contribution on a case-by-case basis, with no clear guidelines for doing so.

As Table 6.2 shows, 22 programs can reduce as well as deny claims when contribution was present. Two programs, in Arizona and Louisiana, can only reduce claims, and 16 deny the entire claim whenever contribution was present.

The standards for contributory conduct also vary; for example, "contributory misconduct" is a more stringent standard than "contribution to the infliction of injury" (Bryant 1990). In fact, a Virginia court determined that, "the provision for reducing the award indicates that the statute has a limited purpose to provide some assistance for those victims or dependents who have no other source of aid," (Virginia Division of Victims Compensation, undated). This suggests that indigent victims—at least in Virginia—should receive some compensation even if they did contribute to their injuries.

Finally, most programs have rules that exempt victims from eligibility if the offender will benefit from the award. However, they cannot simply deny any claim in which the offender is related to or living in the same household with the victim, because VOCA will not fund programs with such sweeping criteria for ineligibility.

In some cases, people other than the victim can be eligible for benefits. Family members of eligible homicide victims, and sometimes of other eligible victims, can be compensated for lost support, counseling, and sometimes replacement services, job training, and other benefits. Many more so-called secondary victims of eligible victims can be compensated for counseling. However, there is no consistent definition of the term secondary victim. Some victim compensation programs limit benefits to people who are both related to and living with the victim, while others require only one of those factors to be present; a few programs make further exceptions.

Benefits generally have a maximum cap, with the exception of New York's program, which pays unlimited medical expenses, but caps all other costs. In addition, most programs set maximum weekly and total income limits, and use payment schedules to contain the costs of medical fees. Thirty-three programs can

Table 6.2
How Compensation Agencies Address Contributory Conduct

STATES THAT REDUCE OR DENY CLAIMS

Alabama	Michigan
Arkansas	Minnesota
California	Missouri
Delaware	Montana
Florida	New York
Georgia	North Carolina
Idaho	Oregon
Indiana	Pennsylvania
Kansas	Rhode Island
Maryland	Virginia
Massachusetts	West Virginia

STATES THAT ONLY REDUCE CLAIMS

Arizona	Louisiana

STATES THAT ONLY DENY CLAIMS

Alaska	New Mexico
Connecticut	North Dakota
Hawaii	Tennessee
Iowa	Texas
Kentucky	Utah
Nebraska	Washington
Nevada	Wisconsin
New Jersey	Wyoming

Note: Data obtained from Parent, Auerbach, and Carlson (1992).

make at least a portion of an award available on an emergency basis, although "emergency basis" can be defined as up to thirty days (Parent, Auerbach, and Carlson 1992). This is hardly helpful if a victim is hungry, faces eviction, or must pay a deposit before a burial is conducted.

Maximum awards are not only methods of cost containment, but set ceilings on practitioner costs, as well. Caps on property reimbursement ensure that essential costs, such as the replacement of clothing held in evidence, will be covered, but that the bulk of funds will be available for medical and wage reimbursement. Rhode Island, one of the few states that makes pain and suffering payments, paid 54 percent of its outlay in 1990 for this category alone, demonstrating how deeply these costs can cut into program resources.

Another crucial factor to consider when evaluating crime victim compensation programs is how their funds are obtained. Since 1984, VOCA has provided matching funds to victim compensation programs, spurring those states without programs to start them. VOCA also mandates certain benefit and eligibility criteria, as well as specialized services for particular types of victims, such as abused children. These mandates limit the spending options of victim compensation programs as they increase their budgets.

The trend in state funding has been to follow the federal model by funding programs through fines levied against offenders, rather than spending public tax dollars to fund compensation programs, although some programs continue to be funded by general revenues instead of or in addition to fines (Parent, Auerbach, and Carlson 1992, Carrow 1980), as shown in Table 6.3. Victim compensation programs also vary as to whether they or another agency are responsible for collecting fines, restitution, and subrogation, and whether they benefit from the results of these collections, as opposed to whether they were simply funded from these collections.

In New York, for example, victim compensation funds come from a Criminal Justice Improvement Account, which collects fines and fees; however, its program's budget is set by the legislature with no regard to the amount of funds in the account. Therefore, New York's victim compensation program would not benefit if its subrogation and restitution collection procedures improved.

In general, victim compensation programs funded by general appropriations turn their own collections back to general appropriations, while those funded by fines and other penalties subrogate their own revenues and keep what they collect. Table 6.3 indicates which sources of funds are tapped by 35 victim compensation programs for which these data were available. Of these, 19 derive their income from fines rather than general revenues, six derive their income from general revenues rather than fines, and eight programs receive funds from both sources. Twenty-seven states derive funds from other sources, as well. For example, Nebraska assesses 5 percent, and New Jersey one-third, of prison inmates' wages.

However, many fines are never collected due to inadequate collection procedures. Across all programs, subrogation accounts for less than 1 percent of program revenues (Parent, Auerbach, and Carlson 1992). Victim compensation programs might improve their collection abilities, however, because the range of collections varies considerably. Three, (New Mexico's, Iowa's and Wyoming's), collected 13 percent, 8 percent and 8 percent of their budgets, respectively, from subrogation proceeds in 1990, suggesting that collection could be improved in other programs, as well.

Another way to consider coverage is to review the "optional" expenses covered by various victim compensation programs. All VOCA-funded programs are required to cover medical and counseling fees, funeral costs, and lost wages, and VOCA provides proportional reimbursement (from fines against federal offenders) for these items. In addition, as shown in Table 6.4, four of the state compensation programs cover pain and suffering, 11 programs cover some types of lost property, 27 programs cover unreimbursed lost wages, 27 programs cover attorneys' fees, 30 programs cover replacement services, and 36 programs cover rehabilitation. These programs clearly offer broader coverage than those in states

Table 6.3
Sources of Income for Victim Compensation Programs

STATE	GENERAL REVENUES	OFFENDER FINES	VOCA FUNDS	OTHER SOURCES
Alabama	X	X	X	X
Alaska		X	X	
Arizona			X	X
Arkansas			X	X
California		X	X	
Connecticut		X	X	X
Delaware		X	X	X
Florida		X	X	X
Idaho		X	X	X
Iowa		X	X	X
Kansas		X	X	X
Kentucky		X	X	X
Maryland	X		X	
Massachusetts	X		X	
Michigan		X	X	X
Minnesota	X	X	X	X
Missouri		X	X	X
Montana		X	X	
Nebraska	X		X	X
Nevada		X		X
New Jersey	X	X	X	X
New York	X	X	X	X
N. Carolina	X		X	
N. Dakota	X		X	
Oklahoma		X	X	X
Oregon	X	X	X	X
Pennsylvania	X	X	X	
Rhode Island		X	X	X
S. Carolina	X	X	X	X
Tennessee	X	X	X	
Texas		X	X	X
Virginia		X	X	X
Washington		X	X	X
Wisconsin	X		X	
Wyoming		X	X	X

Note: Data obtained from Parent, Auerbach, and Carlson (1992), updated by author.

that do not offer these optional services. Another way to consider optional expenses is to note in Table 6.4 that seven programs cover five expenses not mandated by VOCA, 10 cover four, 14 cover three, 11 cover two, and New Mexico covers only one nonmandated cost; or that 14 percent of programs cover five expenses not mandated by VOCA, 32 percent cover at least four, 62 percent cover at least three, and 84 percent cover at least two.

LIMITATIONS OF CRIME VICTIM COMPENSATION

Perhaps the most valid criticism of crime victim compensation is that it accurately reflects society's confusion about victims and their needs. In this way, it contributes to its own perceived ineffectiveness. By funding programs that raise the public's awareness of victims' needs, victim compensation agencies tend to make victims and those who work with them most directly dissatisfied with the status quo.

Those who work toward social change never feel that change occurs rapidly enough. One function of all government agencies is to moderate among factions so changes are made with a reasonable level of consensus. While this process ensures that all sides will have input into change, it also slows the pace of that change.

Chappell (1972) concluded that victim compensation programs in Australia were "political placebos" because of their low maximum payments, limited operational reach, cumbersome delivery system that deterred applications, and focus on those who suffered direct physical injuries. While most victim compen sation programs in the United States have moved beyond Australia's early level of provision, they still reflect these problems to a considerable extent.

And, as noted in Chapter 1, the low level of operation of victim compensation programs is particularly ironic because it contradicts the definition of "compensation." This problem is not unique to American programs, as Chappell's 1972 analysis proves. In fact, in order for Jews persecuted by the Nazis to receive compensation from the German government, they have had to prove that they were confined in a concentration camp for at least six months or in a ghetto or in hiding for at least eighteen months (Binder 1992).

Even if these conflicts were reconciled, the hurdle of implementation would have to be faced, and implementation of victim compensation programs can often be poor and deviate from the intentions of those who advocated for the program (Chambers, Wedel, and Rodwell 1992). As Skocpol (1992) demonstrated, Americans' greatest concern about public benefits is not that they are too generous, but that they are unfairly and inefficiently administered. Effective administration, then, could enhance the public's acceptance of crime victim compensation, and thereby facilitate expansion efforts. One remedy might be to eliminate the patron- age system as a means of appointing board members, as many countries, notably England and Germany, did over a century ago.

Table 6.4
Costs Not Mandated by VOCA

State	Rehab. Services	Replace- ment Svc.	Lost Wages	Attorney Fees	Lost Property	Pain & Suffering
INDIANA	X	X	X	X	X	
NEW YORK	X	X	X	X	X	
PENNSYLVANIA	X	X	X	X	X	
WISCONSIN	X	X	X	X	X	
RHODE ISLAND	X	X	X	X		X
WEST VIRGINIA	X	X	X	X		X
HAWAII	X		X	X	X	X
ALASKA	X	X	X	X		
NEW JERSEY	X	X	X	X		
NORTH DAKOTA	X	X	X	X		
SOUTH CAROLINA	X	X	X	X		
ALABAMA	X	X	X		X	
COLORADO	X	X	X		X	
UTAH	X	X	X		X	
NEVADA	X		X	X	X	
NORTH CAROLINA	X		X	X	X	
TENNESSEE	X		X	X		X
ARKANSAS	X	X	X			
ILLINOIS	X	X	X			
OHIO	X	X	X			
OKLAHOMA	X	X	X			
WASHINGTON	X	X	X			
KANSAS	X	X		X		
KENTUCKY	X	X		X		
TEXAS	X	X		X		
MASSACHUSETTS	X	X		X		
CONNECTICUT	X		X	X		
MARYLAND	X		X	X		
NEBRASKA	X		X	X		
DELAWARE		X	X	X		
LOUISIANA		X			X	
MICHIGAN	X	X				
MINNESOTA	X	X				
OREGON	X	X				
CALIFORNIA	X			X		
MONTANA	X			X		
FLORIDA	X		X			
VIRGINIA		X				
WYOMING		X				
IOWA		X				
IDAHO				X		
MISSOURI				X		
NEW MEXICO	X					
TOTAL	**36**	**30**	**27**	**26**	**11**	**4**

Note: Data obtained from the 1988/1989 *NOVA Legislative Directory* (1990), updated by author.

Politicization of social programs often results in low-level goals being substituted for ones that would be more effective, but that are more expensive or threaten established patterns (Galper 1975). Victim compensation programs can be seen as obfuscating issues governments would rather not address, such as the root causes of crime and its differential effects on various population groups; ignoring the long-term effects of family violence; minimizing the emotional trauma caused by crime, especially to "secondary" victims; and, by its focus on "violent" crime, negating the actions of white collar criminals whose corruption perpetuates the inequities at the core of so many social ills (Reiman 1984).

In addition, by focusing on the vulnerability of victims, victim compensation programs deflect focus from those social institutions that create vulnerable conditions, as well as from those that incite violence in their members. In fact, if victim compensation programs were to truly compensate victims, they would apportion costs, and blame, more broadly, against institutions as well as individuals when appropriate. For example, they might sanction government agencies that fail to protect or report crimes in their jurisdictions. Karmen (1991) noted that such "institution-blaming" is an alternative to both victim-blaming and offender-blaming, which is more sophisticated than either individually oriented alternative because it considers the root causes of violence and victimization.

OPTIONS FOR IMPROVING CRIME VICTIM COMPENSATION

The experience of nearly 30 years of victim compensation program operation has yielded considerable information that can be used to improve them. For example, information on the range of program models and procedures used by these programs offers options to agencies that find their present operation less than optimal. Shared information also gives impetus for programs to alter their operations and provides data to convince policy makers to implement these changes.

Gates (1980) noted that timeliness is a critical factor in resource provision. As noted, states differ in how quickly they provide benefits, and only California's program sets deadlines for claims determination. Providing means-tested emergency awards is the primary way that programs make timely awards to those victims who need them most desperately. However, emergency awards are capped at fairly low levels by all programs, leaving some victims with high costs to wait two years or more for full compensation.

Awards could be made in a more timely way if resources, including compensation funds, staffing, and technology, were expanded in accordance with defined need. In addition to prioritizing the poor through means tests, programs might prioritize victims who suffer severe, costly injuries and victims with no collateral resources, such as insurance or eligibility for other benefits. Furthermore, emergency awards might be offered periodically, to accommodate those victims with high costs who have to wait long periods for claims to be settled. It would be preferable, however, if all claims were determined within a reasonably short time, such as California's 90-day deadline, making many emergency awards unnecessary. Agencies might further conserve their resources if they defined eligibility so that victims who could afford private insurance, but chose not to purchase it, would receive less compensation than victims who were poor or otherwise unable to purchase it.

All state crime victim compensation agencies also fund outreach programs to assist crime victims in obtaining reimbursement and other services. These programs differ in whether they are private, not-for-profit or government-sponsored, and whether they serve all types of crime victims or are targeted to specific victim subgroups. In general, government-based programs tend to serve broader groups of victims, while not-for-profits are more likely to focus on subgroups such as elderly victims, rape victims, or members of a single ethnic or other minority group.

Outreach programs also differ in how they reach out to victims—and when. Some programs that rely heavily on referrals from other agencies experience a time lag from the occurrence of crimes to the time that they make contact with victims. This time lag contributes to the delay victims experience in filing for and obtaining benefits. It is probably best for programs to rely on referrals from hospitals and the police, who have contact with victims soon after the crime, rather than to rely on referrals from district attorney's offices and probation departments, which enter the process later.

Piven and Cloward (1993) demonstrated that keeping people from accessing financial aid programs is the main method by which administrators keep costs down and ward off public attacks against their programs. This is done by maintaining a low agency profile and by complicated eligibility rules and application procedures. Another adaptation of this is failing to provide all that claimants are entitled to, by simply not informing them that they might be entitled to more than they request, either from the agency to which they are applying or from another source. Sometimes this is done to preserve agency resources, and other times out of ignorance of alternatives.

But failing to train staff members about benefits available from other agencies, or from private actions such as civil litigation, can ultimately be costly for agencies, as when they pay for services that would have been covered by another source or when they lose a source of subrogation. In addition, staff burnout increases when workers are unable to help people who come to them for assistance, but lessens when workers learn of alternative ways to serve them (Edelwich 1980, Maslach 1978).

Victim compensation programs could also make greater efforts to improve their visibility. They might do so by creating simplified application processes and manuals outlining program guidelines, eligibility guidelines, and victims' rights. These would be particularly helpful for victims who tend to use other social services, and who might not learn of victim compensation without outreach directed toward their helpers. Such victims include those who are physically, mentally, or developmentally disabled, recent immigrants and others who do not speak fluent English, and members of other groups with special needs. It would, therefore, be beneficial for programs to develop outreach materials directed to traditional helpers, who include social workers as well as clergy and other lay advocates.

Outreach would also be facilitated if some information were printed in foreign languages and in large print, and recorded on audiotape. State-specific material might be augmented by information, perhaps developed by the federal Office for Victims of Crime, for use by all victim compensation programs, which in more general terms explained such issues as the experience of victimization, victim rights, and court procedures. This information could also be offered on the Internet, where agencies as well as individuals could access it, and where people with sight limitations could have information verbalized for them by software that is often available to them as an entitlement.

Victim advocates, funded by victim compensation or other agencies, can also help to meet the special information needs of particular victim groups. Ethnic and race-specific programs, for example, can inform their constituencies of victim services, and can help victims to fill out forms, obtain documentation, and cut through "red tape" that victims might otherwise be unable to negotiate. Some of these programs offer special services needed by the populations they serve, such as transportation for adolescents and seniors or shelter for victims of domestic violence.

Sensitivity to special populations is a more nebulous factor. Nonetheless, services designed for gay and lesbian victims, for example, ensure that they will not avoid help for fear of stigma.

Another outreach method that has proven successful in those programs that utilize them, such as Kansas's and New Jersey's, are statewide hotlines. The greater availability and lower cost of "800" numbers make them a feasible means of getting information about victim compensation quickly and easily to anyone who requests it.

Victim compensation programs were designed to resemble private and social insurance systems, focusing on the use of "people-sustaining technologies," which attempt to prevent, maintain, and retard the deterioration of the welfare or well-being of clients, but do not attempt to change their personal attributes (Hasenfeld 1983). However, changes in victim compensation programs' services, particularly in paying for counseling and other "soft" services, suggest that they also need some staff members to be skilled in "people changing technologies" (Hasenfeld 1983), to help those victims most severely affected by crimes overcome their emotional trauma.

This is also true because, since the early 1980s, social service allocations have been drastically reduced. As a result, the demands on the resources of all social programs, including victim compensation programs, have soared as individuals who have lost benefits on which they had been dependent scramble to qualify for alternative services. Many of these claimants are homeless, deinstitutionalized mental patients or drug abusers.

While these claimants may not be entitled to victim compensation benefits, the emergency nature of their needs, their multiple problems, and the difficulty of determining their eligibility tax victim compensation programs' resources. These claimants are most draining of the time and skills of staff trained in claims investigation, but not in dealing with troubled individuals. This inability frustrates workers, excludes the neediest clients, and leads to systematic neglect of those most in need of help, because the capacity to make use of help is itself a mark of strength (Galper 1975).

Victim compensation programs might add case managers, who could advise clients who have not come to them through victim assistance programs about what to expect regarding their level of entitlement and processing times. Case managers could apprize all applicants of the alternatives and additional options for compensation they might have, such as other benefits and entitlements, private insurance, and civil lawsuits. Case managers could also coordinate with other agencies, so clients would not feel abandoned when referred to workers' compensation, Medicaid, or other benefits providers. Case managers would be particularly helpful in handling walk-in claimants who must be denied emergency awards or be turned away entirely. This would improve public perceptions of victim compensation programs, because people would receive more information earlier and expectations would not be raised inappropriately.

Case management staff could be augmented by student interns from local social work, criminal justice, law, and paralegal programs. This would be a cost-effective way of reducing the workloads of investigators while improving the effectiveness of programs, and it would expand the services of victim compensation programs, rather than transferring the existing functions of staff members to other workers. Internships would also tap the expertise of the various disciplines that relate to crime victims and prepare future professionals for this expanding human service field.

Victim compensation programs might also extend their advocacy services. Kuh (1966) found that victims' primary complaint was that they were denied participation in the criminal justice system. Of course, mechanisms for victim participation have been expanded since then. However, victims tend to be alienated by their actual experiences with the system (Elias 1993). Instead of focusing on rights at trial (because most cases are plea-bargained) or at sentencing and parole (because most offenders are not caught) (Karmen 1991), victim advocates might focus on expanding compensation, restitution, and plea-bargaining rights, which are exercised more often.

Victim compensation programs might also rethink their means of allocating reduced awards to victims. Rather than reducing claims by percentages, they might limit payment to medical and funeral payments when some "fault" is assessed, or conversely, they might provide pain and suffering payments, but limit them to those victims who can prove that they in no way contributed to their injuries.

Before doing so, however, victim compensation programs should develop clear definitions of "contributory conduct," and apply them uniformly. Some critics of these programs consider all contributory conduct rules unnecessarily punitive. This, however, assumes that anyone who calls himself or herself a victim is one.

Karmen (1991) analyzed contributory conduct, noting that "blameworthy" actions of victims can be categorized in three distinct ways:

victim facilitation: making the criminal's task easier by neglecting security precautions
victim precipitation: risk-taking behavior on the part of the victim an
victim provocation: inciting acts that instigate violent responses

Perhaps these distinctions could serve as a guide for victim compensation programs in assessing contributory conduct. Thus, provocation might result in total denial of benefits, while precipitation and facilitation might result in no more than a reduction of benefits.

However, victim compensation programs would better serve society if they publicized information on how facilitation occurs, so potential victims could be warned to take preventive measures to avoid victimization, rather than be punished for failing to take preventive measures. Furthermore, precipitation should be evaluated as a mitigating factor (as insanity is considered to mitigate criminal conduct) because it is often a sign of prior victimization or mental illness.

Several victim populations fall outside of many victim compensation programs' eligibility criteria altogether. Although their numbers cannot be quantified, it appears that some family members of victims who do not live in the same state as the victim are ineligible for compensation because of residency requirements that assume that the victim and the claimant are the same person. Adults who were victimized as children are often unable to receive compensation because of deadlines on reporting requirements and statutes of limitation.

Perhaps the most bitter debate involves the eligibility of battered women and rape victims who do not report their assaults to the police. Advocates argue that theirs are special circumstances that call for different eligibility criteria; opponents challenge that they are not victims if they do not press charges, and that battered women are entitled to services from departments of social services in any case. A policy question that this debate leaves unanswered is whether advocates are helping or harming these victims by supporting their fears of confronting their assailants. Since many of the staff members of these programs were themselves victims of the same crimes, they may be motivated more by their own unresolved conflicts than by the needs of the victims they serve.

Furthermore, it is often economics that traps women in violent households (Elias 1993). Therefore, ensuring that women have economic means and adequate safe, permanent housing for escape are prerequisites to reducing wife abuse, but this is beyond the scope of victim compensation programs.

The requirement that victims report their crimes to the police to be eligible for compensation enables victim compensation investigators to objectively determine that a crime has been committed. But only one-third of all victims report their crimes to the police (United States Department of Justice 1988b). In some cases, too, the police refuse to take reports of crimes, especially from victims they consider "illegitimate," such as prostitutes, people under the influence of drugs, victims of domestic violence, and illegal aliens (Roth 1974). In affluent areas, many violent crimes are not recorded by the police, because these localities prefer not to have records of violence within their borders. Conversely, it appears to be easier to make false police reports in urban areas with high crime rates, where the police do not have the time or staff to investigate each report or to punish false reporters.

Research has demonstrated that compensation has not resulted in any increase in reporting for any crime or in any jurisdiction (Elias 1983), because victims' reasons for not reporting crime are unrelated to the potential receipt of compensation (Kidd and Chayet 1984). In addition, 40 percent of the crimes reported to the police are reported by someone other than the victim (United States Department of Justice 1988b). This suggests that the reporting requirement should be rethought. If compensation is to encourage reporting, and not simply reward it, time should be allowed for victims to report after becoming aware of compensation, and outreach efforts should extend beyond requiring the police to inform victims of victim compensation.

At the very least, compensation should be extended to those victims of domestic violence who report their crimes to other representatives of the criminal justice system, such as family court judges and court officers. Communities might also experiment with anonymous reporting, particularly of sex crimes. While it has obvious limitations, anonymous reporting can alert the police to criminals who use similar methods or locations for their crimes without divulging the identities of victims who choose not to be identified.

Most states justify the reporting requirement by stating that it is federally mandated. Ironically, this may not be the case. Sec. 1403(b)(2) of the Victim Compensation and Assistance Act of 1984 states that

A [state] crime victim compensation *program* is an eligible compensation *program* for the purposes of this section if . . . such a program *promotes* victim cooperation with the reasonable requests of law enforcement authorities [italics added]. (United States Department of Justice 1984a)

The above statement does not specifically require that each victim report the crime against him or her to receive compensation, or even that each victim assistance program encourage its clients to report. It simply requires that state victim compensation programs "promote. . . victim cooperation," which might be construed, for example, as encouraging police agencies to improve their treatment of victims so more are willing to report crimes and cooperate with the police. It remains to be seen whether this law will be reinterpreted, particularly in light of the Clinton administration's interest in crimes against women.

Some secondary victims have been recognized by compensation legislation, but have differential access to services. While spouses are entitled to counseling, for example, members of unmarried couples are not, regardless of the length or nature of their relationships. This is particularly discriminatory against homosexuals who cannot legally marry, and have increasingly been targets of bias-related violence. It will be interesting to observe whether victim compensation programs follow the trend toward extending benefits to gay and lesbian partners, which has recently been noted in regard to corporate benefit plans (Matthews 1993). Even if this were done, however, a determination would have to be made of how to identify a gay or lesbian partner. Would a state pay anyone who claims to be, or to have been, the partner of a crime victim, or would prior registration as a couple (if available in that state) be required? And how might a gay partner be identified in a jurisdiction without partner registration? Is shared payment of household bills adequate, or do both names have to be on a mortgage or lease? How would unmarried heterosexual couples be treated under the same circumstances? Victim compensation programs should review their definitions of secondary victims to ensure that none are being inadvertently overlooked.

If these and other "special" groups of victims are to be equitably compensated, however, victim compensation programs will have to develop nonstigmatizing means of collecting data on the factors that place victims in these groups. This might be facilitated by victim advocates, who could explain the reasons that these data were being collected. Programs also need to differentiate between claims based on primary and secondary victimizations in order to determine how many crimes go uncompensated.

Secondary victims, even of murder, are not entitled to reimbursement of income lost when attending the trial of their loved one's assailant. But such attendance is important, because the family serves the court as a reminder of the deceased victim. Extending lost income to this group would increase public under-standing of the effects of murder on the family, and would not amount to a significant increase in claims because, contrary to public perception, murder trials are quite infrequent (Karmen 1990). Similarly, lost income should be made available to victims who testify at parole hearings, because without such reimbursement, many victims are unable to afford to exercise their right to be heard by judges and sentencing officials.

Still other victims are denied particular services due to technicalities. For example, if renters' doors or windows are damaged, they are usually unreimbursable because they are the landlord's responsibility to repair, even though it is the renters who suffer if landlords delay or refuse to make repairs. Yet data indicate that fully 61 percent of crime victims rent their homes (United States Department of Justice 1988b).

Another difficulty is that some victims forget or deny victimizations for long periods of time, thereby challenging statutes of limitations and making it difficult to budget for this expense (Parent, Auerbach, and Carlson 1992). Such victims of terror, or "long-term" victims, include victims of child abuse and battering, as well as hostages and victims of torture. Survivors of the Holocaust and many other refugees also fall into this group. Some victims of terror cannot distinguish between safety and danger, and are far more frequently victimized than the general population.

Many of these people were victimized long before victim services became available, and before attitudes about female victims of sexual abuse and the veracity of incest victims had improved. Few of these people are eligible for compensation any longer, if they ever were. This is true because most of these cases were not reported to the police at the time, and few police agencies will take a report of a crime so long after the fact that it can no longer be investigated. Moreover, no government agency can provide benefits prior to the date that those benefits were legally initiated, but many of these crimes occurred before the victim compensation agencies the victims must apply to were created - or before those agencies compensated sexual assault victims for counseling expenses.

These victims characteristically repress or deny their traumatic experiences for years and even decades, although most victim compensation agencies limit counseling to injuries "causally related to the crime." This criterion fails to reflect the fact that substance abuse, marital disruptions, eating disorders, and a host of other dysfunctional behaviors have been proven to result from unresolved victimizations, albeit in a more distantly related manner (Lifton 1980). Furthermore, causality of long-repressed trauma is often one of the last factors that can be determined during mental health treatment.

These victims' needs should be addressed specifically. Specialized programs should be directed toward them, and outreach and training should be targeted to the staffs of programs for refugees, substance abusers, anorectics, bulemics, criminals, and other populations that have high proportions of victims. However, these victims would be best served not by expanding victim compensation to them, but by providing universal mental health coverage, which would not require advance determinations of causality to anyone who feels the need for such services (see Chapter 8).

Victims would prefer compensation to be paid for by their assailants (Antilla 1986, Shapland 1986, Carrow 1980), although this does not take into account that most assailants are never caught. If they are, many cannot afford to pay restitution; when it is ordered, restitution often goes unpaid, although it is generally deducted from compensation claims in advance. While most victim compensation programs are now funded by offender fines, no research has determined whether this satisfies victims, or whether they would still prefer to be compensated by the particular person who victimized them. If the latter proves true, replacing compensation with restitution as often as possible would appear to be the ideal alternative to compensation, when it is feasible. It is unlikely, however, that restitution will ever completely supplant the need for victim compensation, as discussed in Chapter 2.

SUMMARY

Crime victim compensation programs were developed to fill a recognized need. Funded primarily by offender fines in most jurisdictions and on the federal level, but provided to victims even if their assailants are not caught or are unable to pay restitution, victim compensation acts as a more effective, timely conduit of offender funds to victims than restitution has proven to be. However, crime victim compensation funds are still very limited and skewed toward particular victim groups and payment categories. Narrow eligibility requirements leave many other victim needs unmet, even when victims obtain all of the victim-specific compensation to which they are entitled.

NOTES

1. This term is often used by conservative victim advocates, although it actually refers to rights of the accused. These rights protect the public from victimization by the criminal justice system, by preventing innocent people from being convicted of crimes while the guilty go free. They are, therefore, a cornerstone of victims' rights, although conservatives who try to use the victims' movement to erode the rights of the accused fail to acknowledge this fact.

2. Victims must have been physically injured or be over 60, under 18, or disabled to receive this reimbursement.

3. An important distinction here is whether clients recall incidents spontaneously, after their defenses are lowered by subsequent trauma or being put at ease by their therapists, or whether therapists "suggest" the cause, and clients "accept" it. Often in the latter case, the therapists demonstrate a pattern of "suggesting" abuse to clients without assessing other possibilities.

7

Recommendations for Improving Victim Reimbursement

Many benefits exist to help victims meet the costs incurred by crime. However, none of these methods covers all of victims' needs in even most circumstances, and meeting needs more fully often involves obtaining benefits and services from a number of disparate sources.

Furthermore, the criminal justice system often vies with crime victims for resources and situational definitions, and tends to treat victims monolithically when they are dealt with at all. This chapter will review the pragmatic and conceptual difficulties inherent in crime victim reimbursement and offer specific recommendations for reducing these difficulties and enabling more victims to be reimbursed more fully and quickly using more simplified procedures. It will also recommend ways that benefit systems and criminal justice agencies can increase and conserve their resources to better meet the various needs of victims of crime.

COST CONTAINMENT AND REVENUE ENHANCEMENT

Any expansion of victim reimbursement mechanisms will require expanded resources. And while, as noted, these resources may be easier to justify than some other public benefits because they are derived primarily from offenders' fines, they still must be carefully allocated. One way to demonstrate this care is to develop cost containment methods for resources that are expended.

To date, most benefit agencies have limited their cost-containment methods to fee schedules and capping. However, there appear to be other ways in which they could further control costs, which offer additional benefits, such as focusing on effectiveness as well as cost control. These agencies might, as some few have, monitor treatment plans, develop peer review committees to oversee counseling, limit payments to qualified professionals who use modalities of treatment appropriate to work with victims, and hire care managers to ascertain that all treatment paid for by the agency is necessary and appropriate.

Furthermore, oversight services should be available to all crime victims, not only those compensated by the monitoring agency. Such monitoring is particularly important today, because health maintenance organizations (HMOs) often lack mental health and even medical staff knowledgeable in how to work with victims, and their case managers often curtail treatment according to arbitrary schedules rather than consideration of case specifics.

Checks should be conducted of all service providers to ensure that all of the services they provide are necessary, and that they are qualified to provide them. While most benefit agencies have investigators or specialists determine medical charges in this way, counseling costs, funeral expenses, and attorneys' fees do not appear to be similarly monitored by most agencies. Not only might this save money, it could generate income if agencies were empowered to fine, and collect the fines from, providers who improperly treat or charge benefit agency third-party payers or crime victims themselves. And it is a very appropriate role for victim reimbursement agencies to protect victims from professional malpractice.

Overuse of benefits is characteristic of health care costs paid for by third parties, because service recipients have no incentive to restrain their consumption (Pinkerton 1995), and service providers have no disincentive to overtreat. These factors contributed to massive health care expenditures in the United States, totaling $884 billion in 1993, or $3,500 for each American (Pinkerton 1995). In fact, only 5 percent of all hospital costs and fewer than 25 percent of all health care costs were paid for out of pocket in that year (Pinkerton 1995).

Part of this problem can be attributed to what Robert Samuelson has defined as "the politics of overpromise." Samuelson observes that governments systematically and routinely make more commitments than they can fill, often to discrete or even conflicting constituencies. These "overpromises" give the public a sense of entitlement to the promised benefits. Unfortunately, most agencies have insufficient resources to meet all the demands made of them. As a result, they are forced to limit outreach, set arcane rules, create delays, and take other "gatekeeping" actions to limit access to their insufficient, overpromised resources (Samuelson 1995).

These facts, coupled with the increased concern that government benefits should not undermine personal responsibility, suggest that all benefits, including those targeted to crime victims, should be rethought. While most Americans agree with the overall goal of reimbursing victims, there is little understanding of the methodologies of these programs, and less of how they reflect the various theories of benefit provision.

To give victim compensation benefits the advantage of broad, popular support, efforts should be made to make redistribution as direct as possible, and to ensure that personal responsibility is supported, rather than undermined. This last could be facilitated by increasing emphasis on prevention, providing some benefits to victims even if they have other resources, and offering some additional benefits to victims who are judged blameless.

Overtreatment and overuse carry dangers other than economic ones, as well. Overtreatment can cause iatrogenic medical problems, and can make victims overly dependent on service providers (particularly in the case of mental health services). This problem is exacerbated in the face of new, costly technologies and equipment, which doctors and hospitals are eager to pay off. For example, although no one has yet determined a "safe" number of NMRI (nuclear magnetic resonance imaging) tests that a person can sustain over a lifetime, many doctors have been found to prescribe NMRIs with little concern about overexposure to them.

Fraud is rampant in public benefits, costing up to 10 percent of all allocations, according to Medicare fraud experts. Claimants, too, may be defrauding benefit agencies, either through false reports of crimes (hard fraud) or by "padding" otherwise legitimate claims (soft fraud). Investigators believe that as much as $346 million has been paid to people who made false claims against federal agencies alone in recent years (Valente 1995).

Insurance experts have learned that many people feel justified in committing such fraud, because they feel that private and governmental benefits agencies overcharge and overtax them for these services (Crenshaw 1993). It should be recalled that exaggerated claims by victims were the historic reason that governments initially became involved in the compensation process. In particular, some victims may be "double dipping," or receiving multiple payments for the same injuries. This can occur because compensation agencies often fail to determine whether victims are eligible for alternative benefits, and to collect subrogatable funds such as restitution payments that they had advanced to victims.

Collection of subrogation appears to be most effective when the agency responsible for its collection directly benefits from the proceeds. Therefore, empowering benefit agencies to conduct both tasks—and retain the proceeds—could facilitate higher levels of collection and ensure that proceeds are keyed to victims' needs. This might be facilitated by reinstating the ancient system of charging offenders damages that constitute three times their victims' costs. Victims would then receive one-third, exactly what they had expended, which would discourage false claims based on the hope of excessive compensation. The second third would be allocated to administrative costs and the final third to general funds to compensate society—the *really* forgotten victim in the compensation process. The inverse of this is that the government obtains millions of dollars in civil forfeitures, but little of that money is ever funneled to victims (Heilbroner 1994).

Benefits programs could enhance victims' receipt of reimbursement and control their own costs by screening compensation claims for factors that would make restitution or civil litigation particularly likely to result in payments to victims, and by helping them to access these payments. This might include revising notoriety-for-profit legislation and other civil litigation to permit uncollected funds to go to a general fund for victims. In particular, separate determinations could be made for compensatory damages, payable only to victims or their survivors, and punitive damages, which could be distributed to victims more broadly, or earmarked for educational or preventive purposes.

Increasing the use and amount of restitution would also offset victim compensation programs' costs, and raise their revenues by increasing the pool of funds they could subrogate. This could be expanded to "advancing" victims money, which would later be reimbursed through subrogation. (This might be an answer to the dilemma of "unjust enrichment," in which compensation agencies deny benefits to battered spouses because their abusers are responsible for their medical care.) And, as the bulk of victim compensation funds are derived from offender fines rather than tax dollars, greater efforts should be made to ensure that these funds are tapped before victims are relegated to tax-funded government benefits. This suggests that the low overall caps of many state crime victim compensation agencies should be raised.

It must be reiterated, however, that victim compensation agencies must not design their programs to supplant these civil remedies, however, as workers' compensation does, because that would only limit victims' reimbursement options. Instead, they should focus on providing timely, basic compensation to meet victims' needs while victims investigate other avenues of reimbursement.

THE DILEMMA OF DEFINING VICTIMS' NEEDS

The relative infancy of victim compensation and the dearth of information on victims' needs and how to meet them, have given rise to various advocacy efforts to expand victims' rights and to improve services and resources available to victims. Groups advocating for these rights include victims, professionals who work with victims, and sometimes benefit programs themselves. Yet these groups often have disparate goals, as well as disparate views of victims' needs.

For example, victim efforts to "Take Back the Night," programs in which victim groups fill the streets to demonstrate that those streets belong to the public rather than to criminals, are meaningless exercises because they do nothing to make the streets safer the 364 days each year that "Take Back the Night" events do not take place. In fact, demanding the "right" to safety may lead some people to take chances that they otherwise might not, as if the desire for a right, or even the fact of one, negates all possibilities that that right might be infringed upon.

These narrowly focused groups are also worrisome because their single-issue appeals are made to legislators who are increasingly unwilling to take hard positions on substantive policy issues (Gummer 1990). Policy makers often take the easy route of expanding benefits to a limited, but vocal, group rather than assessing which groups are most in need of expanded benefits.

This process exemplifies a deep conflict in attitudes toward policy making: while policy should be informed by expertise, democracy requires responsiveness to interest groups (Lindblom 1980). The danger inherent in this is that when cutbacks are made, they are rarely distributed evenly among recipient groups. Programs serving politically well-organized groups fare better than those without an active constituency. These well-organized groups also have a say in the design of services; so even if they are provided universally, services are most likely to appeal to and benefit special interests (Gilbert 1983).

For example, females and the elderly, who express the greatest fear of crime, but appear to be least at risk, (possibly because domestic violence and sexual assault are less frequently reported than other crimes), have succeeded in obtaining specialized services through targeted funds from VOCA, VAWA and other sources (United States Department of Justice 1988a, Smith and Freinkel 1988). Without doubt, while victim services are generally poorly funded, programs for victims of sexual assault receive the bulk of all victim-directed funds (Sobieski 1991).

Another area where this disparity is clear is in the area of privacy. Most professionals, particularly those in the medical, mental health, and legal fields, are bound by rules requiring them to maintain the confidentiality of the clients they serve. However, particularly in high profile cases, some professionals believe that publicity will be helpful to their cases to the point that they encourage their clients to "go public", and even to "try" their cases before the "court of public opinion."

Individual victims also have diverse views on these issues. Some feel that publicity will pressure the criminal justice system to pay more attention to their cases. And they may be correct, although it should not be necessary to do this in order to obtain the interest or attention of the criminal justice system.

Other victims resent publicity, particularly when the "court of public opinion" views aspects of their personalities or behaviors unfavorably, or when aspects of the crimes against them are stigmatizing. A further variable in these cases is how they cases gained publicity: whether particular victims sought publicity, were thrust into the spotlight by news media or the sensationalism of the case, or were urged to seek publicity by attorneys or other advisors.

The ironies here are clear: What is beneficial to some victims is not necessarily beneficial to others, and what is beneficial to the victims' *movement* may not be best, or even desirable, for particular victims.

For example, the more awareness the public has of the incidence of sexual assault, the less stigmatizing it will become over time. This does not mean, however, that victims who currently speak out will not be stigmatized. More important, circumstances surrounding the crime and the victim's lifestyle will determine the degree of stigma, but the victim may not realize the public's perception of these factors until the media has publicized the case.

The amount of stigma victims feel is also based on the degree of negative connotation they perceive among those close to them (Finkelhor and Associates 1986, Goffman 1963). Therefore, demanding harsher penalties for particular crimes, such as sex crimes, can, in effect, make victims feel more damaged than they otherwise might.

As victimization constitutes a loss of power and control, helping victims to overcome its trauma requires at minimum helping them to regain power and control. Therefore, telling victims to "go public"—or that they need counseling—may be antithetical to victims' interests. Over time, as some victims choose to tell their stories, the stigma of victimization will lessen, because secrecy in itself increases the stigma of victimization (Finkelhor and Associates 1986). And counseling is only helpful when clients are willing participants in the process.

Attempts, however well-meaning, to force this process by encouraging particular victims to give up their privacy against their will, or even against their better judgment, tend to exacerbate victims' trauma. Instead, compensation payments for pain and suffering might be provided to those victims who lose privacy as a result of their public disclosures, especially if their cases go to trial, and most particularly if those trials are televised.

A study of the needs of victims—and of the effectiveness of the mechanisms to meet those needs—is long overdue. It is vital to determine when and how much counseling is necessary—and under what circumstances counseling is not needed or ceases to be effective. Before this is done, however, policy makers and victim advocates must recognize the limits of mental health technologies, and acknowledge that some victims can not be helped, or fully helped, by mental health treatment.

Services to victims must be made more equitable. Currently, victims of sexual assault receive far more services—especially counseling—than victims of other crimes. Secondary victims of homicide, and victims who receive permanent or long-term injuries, should receive services that are at least equal to those received by sexual assault victims, whether that requires decreasing services to the latter or increasing them to the former.

Furthermore, the fragmentation of benefits makes it difficult to determine which victims, and which of their costs, are most effectively met by a combination of public benefits. Unless the agencies that provide these benefits are merged, or their services better coordinated, periodic studies should be conducted to determine the overall equity of public benefits to victims of crime and the degree of coverage of each of their discrete needs.

Another way that victim services might be made more equitable would be to provide some level of government reimbursement to all victims, regardless of whether they have private insurance coverage. Alternatively, indigence, and not just lack of insurance, should be used as a means test. Without such a rule, some victims will obtain benefits only because they failed to purchase private protection that they could afford, while others will be denied benefits only because they were responsible enough to purchase private insurance.

THE CRIMINAL JUSTICE SYSTEM AND VICTIM JUSTICE

There are also underlying conflicts between victims and criminal justice agencies. Not only do they vie for the same resources, as they have since the beginning of history, they also vie for definition and control of circumstances, with victims blaming the criminal justice system for the fact of crime and vice versa.

Victim compensation minimizes and deflects criticism of the criminal justice system and minimizes the social unrest that might develop if the poor (who are most often victims largely because they are forced to live in dangerous neighborhoods filled with other poor, as well as alienated and needy, individuals) were also forced to bear the costs of these crimes, which they could ill afford. This is true despite the low "take up" rates of compensation programs, because nonpayment implies "unworthiness," so that claimants who are denied benefits tend to blame themselves, rather than society, for their failure to obtain compensation (Reiman 1984).

This is exemplified by media focus on victims that distorts and exaggerates the increase in crime. Such actions can backfire on victims as funds that might have been allocated for victim services are diverted instead to criminal justice efforts.

Elias (1993) noted that victim groups have been manipulated into acting on behalf of the criminal justice system. This has blinded them to the needs of most victims, who tend to prefer not to participate in the criminal justice system, and who do not tend to find such participation helpful emotionally or concretely.

One way that this is occurring is in the area of victims' rights legislation. Some of this legislation, which has the expressed purpose of equalizing the balance of justice between victims and offenders, actually undermines the rights of those accused of crimes to be considered innocent until proven guilty (O'Neill 1994, "Victims' Rights" 1992, Karmen 1990, Rudovsky 1988). Ironically, this legislation has not proven to sway judges (Villmoare and Neto 1987), and has even caused the Supreme Court to overturn some convictions on the grounds that the victims' feelings about the crime are not relevant in determining guilt or in sentencing (National Association of Crime Victim Compensation Boards 1991). This determination may appear heartless until one considers the inverse—should offenders be judged *less* guilty because their victims are inarticulate, or have been murdered and have no loved ones to represent them?

Karmen (1991) noted that the so-called victims' movement may be more of a "law and order" movement that coopts victims to support its (not victims') agendas. Elias (1992) suggested that this belief is exemplified by increases in prison construction, incarceration, sentences, preventive detention, and capital punishment, none of which has resulted in declines in victimization rates.

Another example of this is the criminal justice system's recent use of civil forfeiture. The government had been using confiscation laws, originally designed to reduce the resources of organized criminals, to divert other offenders' resources for its own use. Offenders' funds confiscated by the government could then not be tapped by victims for restitution—and were rarely allocated in significant amounts to victims by any other means (Heilbroner 1994). And, although a federal appeals court ruled that the government cannot pursue both criminal and civil complaints against the same offenders, as doing so constitutes double jeopardy (Goldberg 1996), its ruling was overturned by the Supreme Court ("Justices Uphold" 1996).

Elias (1993) noted that we are not only a culture of violence, but "a culture of violent solutions." Yet our violent solutions result in even higher rates of violence. Certain but lesser punishment and availability of treatment are actually more effective crime deterrents (Box-Grainger 1986). Moreover, police work would be more effective if it consisted of preventing the causes of crime (Elias 1993) by working with community organizations, which are more effective in promoting the kinds of social order that lead to reduced crime (Currie 1985).

What might benefit victims most, and is essentially what most victims (although not necessarily the most vocal victims) want, would be to make the criminal justice process less adversarial. This approach would be especially helpful in cases where both participants bear some blame for the altercation (as in a bar fight) or when the participants have an on-going relationship. However, in all criminal cases the adversarial system discourages offenders from admitting guilt or showing remorse.

Witnessing the offender's guilt and remorse is healing to the victim, and helps the victim forgive the offender and put closure on the crime. Restitution has the best chance of being awarded, and paid, when the offender admits guilt and shows remorse, as well. Making the criminal justice system less adversarial, and linking it to restitution, could lead to a re-melding of civil and criminal procedures, so victims would not have to go to court a second time to obtain civil damages. However, for this to occur, hard choices would have to be made: Should the strict procedural protections of criminal litigation, the looser requirements of civil procedures, or some combination of the two be used to determine criminal guilt on the one hand and civil fault on the other? Note, too, that this procedure does not incorporate third-party negligence, which would have to be addressed in a separate forum in any case.

Forgiveness may be difficult for victims, but it results in better resolution and healing than does revenge (Henderson 1985). Furthermore, harsh punishments give more power to the government, which has not proven to be the "friend of victims" it purports to be (Brants and Koh 1986). One way to encourage forgiveness, or at least reconciliation, is to recognize how both victims and offenders are victims of circumstances that promote injustice, and that both share an interest in preserving human rights (Elias 1993).

Reimbursement itself can serve as a means of reconciling victims, particularly if the crime was property-based or resulted in only minor injury. Reimbursement demonstrates offenders' willingness to make their victims whole again, which can improve offenders' self-image as well as victims' image of offenders.

With the advent of technological means of tracking offenders, house arrests and orders of protection, which require that offenders keep a distance away from their victims, have become more effective as well as more cost-efficient. These means make it feasible to keep all but the most violent criminals in the community, where they can support their families, pay restitution, and save society the cost of their incarceration. This is particularly important in domestic violence cases, where fear of loss of the offender's income often deters reporting of the abuse.

However, it is vital that restitution not be used to discriminate against poor criminals while keeping higher-income-producing criminals out of prison. In fact, there needs to be more recognition of the fact that white collar crime can be extremely violent, and even homicidal, as class action lawsuits against manufacturers of breast implants, intrauterine devices, and cigarettes, and perpetrators of environmental spills have legally established (Mokhiber 1988). Furthermore, by making the public more aware of the danger of white collar crime it may be possible to reduce racism, because Americans fear street crime (Jencks 1992), which is disproportionately committed by Blacks, more than crimes of the equally violent white collar variety.

The criminal justice system has defined crime in terms of offenders' acts, but to victims, other characteristics or circumstances of crimes, such as the relationship of the victim to the offender or the violence of the act, are often more significant. The criminal justice system defines crimes as assaults, sex crimes, and homicides, for example, but these distinctions say little about the victimizations they represent. Was the assault a gunshot wound that left the victim paralyzed, or a punch in the nose that may have been provoked by ethnic slurs or drunken advances? Was the sex crime "flashing" or a brutal rape? Even homicides can have justifiable elements. If these factors were noted more uniformly and in detail in criminal justice documentation, it would be easier for victim compensation programs to determine contribution and the extent of need for compensation, and for criminal justice researchers to estimate the extent and effects of victimization.

The methodologies of both the Uniform Crime Reports, gathered by the FBI, and the National Crime Survey, conducted by the Bureau of the Census, were recently expanded to incorporate more information on victims (Biderman and Lynch 1991). However, these updates did not include ways to differentiate domestic from non-domestic[1] violence nor to break down types of sex crimes, which would be necessary to determine the extent to which victim compensation reaches victims of these crimes. Furthermore, society views domestic violence as a family problem, not as a societal problem caused by systemic sexism (Elias 1993). Prevention methods would certainly be rethought if the causes of domestic violence (itself a sanitized term for what is usually wife-beating or child-beating) were redefined.

CRIME PREVENTION

Crime is in itself the greatest injustice to victims, for which no form or amount of compensation can ever make up. However, victim compensation programs might use the information they obtain on victimizations to help prevent crimes, by identifying dangerous conditions and locations, for example. The Office for Victims of Crime might even use prevention as a means of allocating VOCA funds. If funding were tied to reducing gun-related violence, for instance, states would have added impetus to address that concern.

However, funds for crime prevention should not be diverted from compensation. Punishing crime is entirely distinct from reimbursing victims, and, while more of one may offset the need for the other in broad ways, prevention does not affect the needs of individuals who are victimized despite prevention efforts.

Many crime victim advocates oppose studies of crime as intrusive to victims and tantamount to "victim-blaming." This is particularly true when those studies seek to identify causes of crime. But it is vitally important that studies regarding the causes of crime be conducted, because their results will determine the best methods of crime prevention.

Studies of the causes of crime demonstrate that most crime is predictable. Usually prediction is based upon the location of the crime; more recently, because of the "revolving door" character of the criminal justice system, coupled with the precipitous and often inappropriate discharge of mental patients from in-patient facilities, prediction has been related to offenders with histories of committing similar crimes under similar circumstances.

However, some predictability can be traced to victims who are unusually trusting or lacking in caution. In most of these cases, the victims are very young, developmentally disabled, or mentally ill, and often they have experienced considerable violence in their lives. Therefore, these victims are far from "asking for it"; instead, they are simply unable to distinguish danger from safety. But desperately needed special services and prevention efforts will not be targeted to these victims until victim advocates are willing to admit that they exist.

One of the easiest ways to reduce crime would be to decriminalize acts that are currently illegal. The largest portion of criminal justice resources are allocated to the detection and prosecution of such crimes as gambling, prostitution, and the use and sale of illicit drugs. These are sometimes referred to as "victimless crimes," although that is clearly a misnomer, as anyone who lives in a neighborhood where drugs or sex are sold can attest. What sets these crimes apart is that they lack complaining witnesses, because all parties to these transactions commit acts considered criminal. Without witnesses to report these crimes, surveillance, wiretapping, undercover work, and other costly means must be employed to detect them (Benjamin and Miller 1991).

Legislation has never been an effective means of enforcing moral behavior. Instead, it drives these crimes underground, where they can neither be taxed nor regulated, and where violence and exploitation are rife. Making "moral" crimes illegal also spurs more crime: thefts to accommodate costs inflated due to illegality; violation of zoning laws because there are no places where these transactions can be legally conducted; and corruption of the police who are supposed to protect the public from these acts (Benjamin and Miller 1991). As these crimes are so common (suggesting a dissonance between society's professed abhorrence and actual participation in them), they clog courts and prisons, creating excuses for leniency toward the most violent offenders.

Paradoxically, decriminalization would protect the public from the worst effects of these crimes. It would reduce "quality of life crimes," which affect others primarily because of their location (and which disproportionately occur in poor, indifferently policed neighborhoods). "Red light districts" and licensing of establishments that provide formerly illegal entertainment could contain these activities far from residential areas and schools.

The decriminalization of prostitution would make the employers of prostitutes responsible for their safety, and if prostitutes were victimized during the course of their employment they would be eligible for workers' compensation. (This would solve the dilemma regarding "contributory conduct" of prostitutes who are victimized while working.) Decriminalization of prostitution would also make it possible to screen prostitutes for AIDS and other diseases. Decriminalization of illicit drugs would make it easier for abusers to seek treatment, because they would not also have to admit to illegal behavior.

Decriminalization would bring these activities and those employed in them into the light of day, where they could be taxed and regulated. The worst forms of exploitation would be reduced, because victims of exploitation would have legal recourse against their employers. As noted, workers would become eligible for benefits based on employment, and the health care costs of their jobs could be evaluated and taxed accordingly.

Decriminalization would also create a new source of taxable funds. Drug sales are estimated at $40 to $50 billion annually (Miller, Cohen and Wiersema 1996). Currently illegal gambling annually adds an additional $120 billion ("Betting Odds" 1995). Add the unknown but considerable cost of illegal prostitution, and it is clear that legalization would broaden the tax base substantially. Note, too, that these figures do not incorporate the savings that would result if the criminal justice system no longer had to prosecute these cases, nor do they reflect the resources, including police officers and jail cells, that would be freed to address violent criminals. The country's recent experience with cigarettes not only suggests that they can be better controlled while legal, but also demonstrates how cigarette companies can be held responsible for the costs of treatment for tobacco addiction as well as the costs of anti-use campaigns and other public education (Kluger 1996).

Finally, our greatest deterrent to crime, and the one most quickly eroding before our eyes, is the First Amendment. In the diversity of America, people must communicate with each other in order to understand each other. Attacks on our First Amendment—by left-wing as well as right-wing activists—close off this communication, sometimes even equating politically incorrect speech with physical violence. In fact, however, these two are polar opposites. If we are to reduce crime, and the fear of crime, we must provide socially acceptable outlets for the expression of difference.

Furthermore, free speech enables the public to identify the attitudes of others. Would the nation have benefitted if David Duke had been denied his right to proclaim himself a Nazi—or did his exercise of free speech openly demonstrate his unfitness for public office? Encouraging public debate and other forms of peaceful dissent are more effective approaches to crime prevention than attempting to squelch all forms of angry expression. Not only are such actions nonviolent, and not criminal, but it is only through dissent that we can hope to achieve both peace and justice, and thereby reduce crime. And crime reduction is far better policy than victim reimbursement in any form.

SUMMARY

Methods of reimbursing victims are increasing, but many problems still exist. Benefit agencies need to contain their costs, increase their resource pools and target increased resources to the most underserved victims. Furthermore, society must improve the ways that victims are served, by benefits agencies and the public, and ensure that all of the legitimate needs of all types of victims of crime are given adequate consideration. In addition, agencies must use the information that they learn about victimization to prevent crimes as well as to deal with their aftermath.

NOTE

1. Currently, the FBI uses the term "domestic crime" in contrast to "street crime," to distinguish where a crime occurred, but not the relationship between the offender and the victim.

8

The Future of
Crime Victim Reimbursement

Even if victim reimbursement mechanisms and criminal justice procedures were improved, victims would continue to face obstacles from the many systems that are not specifically identified as victim (or criminal justice) specific. This final chapter will explore how victim needs might be recognized by the broader system of public and private benefits, and how victim services might be universalized by interweaving them with other benefits into a single, universal health care system, perhaps supplemented by a single wage replacement system and a constellation of smaller agencies designed to address the specific needs of identified subgroups, such as crime victims and elderly and disabled people.

DEVELOPMENT OF UNIVERSAL PROGRAMS

As noted, some victims use helpers who specialize in issues other than victimization, and may, therefore, be unfamiliar with victim services. This is especially the case when victims are elderly, physically or developmentally disabled, or belong to ethnic or other minority groups. Furthermore, some victims prefer not to disclose their victim status. This is particularly true of victims of domestic violence and sexual assault. The best way to serve these victims, and perhaps all victims, is to provide services to them that are not based on victim status.

For example, many victims of domestic violence fail to leave their victimizers because they are not financially able to do so. This is also the reason that many return even after they have left for temporary shelter (Kremen 1984). Access to affordable housing would help them, and would address still another broad social need. And, because financial criteria alone are used to determine eligibility for low-cost housing, victims of domestic violence would not have to identify themselves as such to obtain safe housing. This is critical, because many victims have to feel safe before they can begin to overcome their situations.

All benefit programs that provide medical assistance would become much more efficient if they were freed from the considerable task of assessing eligibility for medical benefits. This could be made possible through universal health care. Such universal programs sustain more widespread public support than victim-specific, or targeted, programs. Universal programs also create greater equality and lessen confusion. Targeted programs are best used to supplement them by addressing issues not addressed by universal programs (Wilson 1987).

With universal health care, eligibility would be determined by medical need alone, and not by the need to fit discrete victim criteria. In this way, it would cover victims for non-crime-related illnesses and injuries, and cover family members of victims who would otherwise lose coverage when victims' jobs—or lives—are lost. It would also cover real, but indirect, costs of crime that are not currently compensable by government victim benefits, such as treatment for alcoholism or attempted suicide precipitated by victimization. Such universalism would require that people pay a reasonable insurance premium, which could be subsidized for the poor. (This would not create a new cost, but would afford new revenues—Medicaid recipients currently receive health care without paying a premium of any kind.)

It should be noted that universal health care and other universal benefits do not have to render private insurance expendable. Private health insurance companies might operate this system for the government, and might also continue to cover optional services for non-life-threatening conditions.

Universal benefits are not more widely accepted in this country in part because many workers currently have generous benefits that they do not want to see compromised. These workers, and other taxpayers, resent paying into government benefit systems they do not anticipate ever having to access.

To counter this, the government might set a specific baseline of health care and wage replacement for which all Americans would be eligible. Employers and individuals could then choose to supplement these benefits through the purchase of private supplemental insurance. For example, the government might guarantee wage replacement at a given standard, such as the poverty line or the median income. Employers could then offer supplemental private insurance to cover the difference between the standard and employees' actual wages. Such a plan would give all taxpayers a stake in the universal benefit system, while retaining a role for private insurers and employers who choose to use generous benefit packages to attract and retain employees. It would also ensure those who could afford it that their economic lifestyles would not have to be altered considerably if they experience a crime that makes them unable to continue earning their present salaries. Nothing would prevent such a system from incorporating deductibles, copayments, and other mechanisms to control costs and overuse, nor from conducting case-specific and broader research to increase crime prevention and public safety.

If universal health care is not implemented, a plan to provide estimated reimbursement to health providers according to past rates of compensation, adjusted periodically, would make it possible to speed compensation to victims. Later, medical reimbursement could be calculated with care and deliberation.

A broader problem addressed neither by proponents of benefit and eligibility cuts nor by redistributional universalists is the responsibility of individuals to insure themselves against potential risks. Government (at all levels) has vast experience with developing and operating mechanisms to collect taxes, garnish wages and otherwise collect and reallocate taxpayer funds. It also has the strength of law on its side. Therefore, the government might collect a portion of income to be allocated to personal insurance premiums, at least in the cases of people who have made no other insurance provisions for themselves. The poor might receive a "credit" toward insurance, similar to the Earned Income Tax Credit, which would enable them to purchase insurance for themselves, as many policy experts have advocated.

The government might even consider assessing a similar levy to collect restitution funds, because so many criminals use indigence to avoid making restitution payments. This could be assessed against all taxpayers, although payment rates would increase only if the payer committed a crime. This benefit could "convert" to a lump-sum retirement benefit at age 65, making it essentially a pension fund that could be tapped preretirement only to pay criminal restitution.

Kahn (1970) noted that specialized access structures can be created to ensure that clients make proper connections with service agencies. Like case management, specialized access systems focus on clients' needs rather than individual agencies' narrow purviews. If it is recognized that many victims' needs for health care and income can be met, or supplemented, by existing agencies, it seems wise to facilitate such access. Perhaps a "gateway" agency, as Kahn envisions, which might act as either an integrative "no fault" social agency or as a case management-oriented referral center to other agencies, might best meet the needs of victims and others who require an array of social services that no single agency can offer.

The core of the inadequacy of victim compensation is the fact that victim status has little to do with the health care, housing, and other basic needs of people who have been victimized by crime. These needs also have little to do with the innocence of victims, or, as in the case of long-term victims who develop a victim orientation, with the closeness in time or detail of mental illness with a "compensable" crime.

As long as the costs of basic needs remain out of the reach of so many people, some will try to avail themselves of services to which they are not entitled, but which they desperately need. Given the societal provision of health care[1] and full employment at decent wages, benefit agencies could be relieved of these expenses and operate more efficiently.

It is now apparent that the administrative costs of health care in the United States are one of the factors making it the most expensive in the world. This text has demonstrated that one reason this cost is so high is that both governmental and private insurers must determine more than the medical necessity for treatment. Unique to the U. S. system of health care is the massive and costly task of analyzing the circumstances that caused an illness or injury, in order to determine which of the array of benefits providers is responsible for covering it. This may have been cost-saving when early, limited benefits were developed. Today, when these benefits appear to meet most of the medical needs of most Americans, the cost of assessing causative factors is a wasteful and unnecessary process that can delay treatment, and therefore increase its cost. Broad provision of health care would limit agencies' need to act as gatekeepers to their services. Relieved of much of this burden and expense, they might become able to more fully provide, and advocate for, the nonmedical needs of victims.

It is also important to recognize, however, that how these systems are implemented, and not the fact of their existence, determines their effectiveness. Critical features such as cost control and sanctions against abuse will be necessary in any such system in order to meet actual needs without bankrupting benefit programs.

Similarly, private insurance would benefit from clarification of its coverage, especially in the case of intentional harm. The private insurance business would also benefit from a clarification of public benefit coverage, so purchasers of private insurance could determine how much they would need to supplement public benefits in order to maintain their lifestyles. (While everyone would not be able to afford to do so, at least people would not be shocked when public benefits force them to reduce their expenses.) Finally, punitive damages should be defined according to a scale constructed so that they become tied to the actual pain and suffering of the victim, and not only the ability of the offender or third-party payer to afford them.

CONCLUSION

The purpose of this text has been to shed light on the range of benefits available to crime victims. In doing so, it has also pointed to the limitations of these benefits and ways that they can be improved. It is hoped that this knowledge will be used to help benefit agencies understand victims' needs and to coordinate their efforts to meet these needs as fully as possible. It is also hoped that it will provide impetus to social workers and others concerned with victims' needs to address the issue of victim compensation with a broader knowledge of victims' needs and alternative ways that they can be met.

Finally, it is hoped that this text will result in expanded and improved services to crime victims. For, while crime victimization remains a cruel but common experience for many, particularly in the United States, the provision of help to victims affirms the public's responsibility and sensitivity to the promotion of a just and humane society.

NOTE

1. There is precedent for this. New Zealand's first attempt at providing victim compensation resulted instead in the provision of universal health benefits. The New Zealand government recognized that medical bills were the chief costs of crime borne by victims (as they continue to be in the United States). By universalizing health care, New Zealand reduced the cost of crime to victims while also addressing a broader social need. Australia and Great Britain followed suit. In Hawaii and Canada, where near-universal and universal health care, respectively, exist, compensation programs rarely need to cover health care costs (Eddy 1992).

Glossary

ADJUSTED COMPENSATION RATE: an estimate of the rate at which state crime victim compensation programs compensate eligible crime victims. The rate is obtained by dividing the total number of violent crimes reported to the FBI by the number of claims paid by all victim compensation programs or on a state-by-state basis, then reduced to 22 percent to reflect Kenneth Carlson's estimate that the remaining 78 percent of cases would be covered by private insurance or other benefits, or would be ineligible due to contributory conduct.

CAPS: maximum payments made by benefit agencies in total or to specific claimants, and maximum amounts payable for specific categories of need, such as medical costs, funeral costs, and wages.

CARLSON ESTIMATES: see ADJUSTED COMPENSATION RATE.

CIVIL LITIGATION: noncriminal, "tort," or contract-infringement cases, which can be brought by victims against offenders and negligent third parties who were responsible for the occurrence of crimes. See also INDEMNIFICATION.

COMPENSABILITY: the degree to which financial costs can be compensated by a benefit program, after determining that the costs are reasonable, do not exceed caps placed on those costs, are unrecoverable from other sources, and are reimbursable by the specific program.

COMPENSATION: a principle of benefit allocation that reflects a systemic failure or "debt" on the part of a government for failing to prevent harm it is empowered to prevent.

CONTRIBUTORY CONDUCT: actions by the victim that may have provoked, precipitated, facilitated, or caused the crime to be committed, and that make the victim ineligible for compensation.

COVERAGE: the degree to which a particular cost is reimbursable by a particular benefit agency.

ELIGIBILITY: factors determining whether a claimant can receive compensation from a particular benefit agency.

EMERGENCY AWARDS: portions of awards made by some state crime victim compensation programs in a very short time. Means-tested, they are designed to ensure that the poorest claimants can meet their crime-caused expenses in a timely way.

INDEMNIFICATION: payment owed for action already taken. Refers to the concept that offenders obligate themselves to reimburse victims by the criminal acts that create these costs.

NEED: want of the means of subsistence. This term can be variously defined.

NOTORIETY-FOR-PROFIT LEGISLATION: sometimes called "Son of Sam" laws after the criminal whose planned book depicting his crimes was the cause of the legislation, these laws ensure that victims will be able to collect damages against their offenders from sales of the depictions of their crimes, as well as other funds the offender may have or may obtain.

OFFENDERS' RIGHTS: a term used to disparage the rights of accused persons. These rights are actually another form of victims' rights, because they help to ensure that innocent persons are not convicted of crimes while guilty parties go free.

PAIN AND SUFFERING: sometimes intangible results of criminal injuries, which are rarely paid by public benefit programs, but often in response to civil litigation.

REPARATION: reimbursement to victims of military conflicts.

RESTITUTION: payments made to victims directly by their offenders to compensate them for losses sustained as a result of crimes.

RESTORATION: returning victims to their former (precrime) states.

SECONDARY VICTIMS: family members or other persons close to a crime victim who suffer emotionally, and possibly financially, as a result of crime.

SERVICE RESTITUTION: often referred to as "community service," this refers to methods by which offenders "work off" their debts to undo damage they caused.

SOCIAL WELFARE PROGRAMS: the broad array of benefits and services, each with its own eligibility factors and benefit levels, that are provided by federal and state governments to meet various socially recognized needs.

"SON OF SAM" LAW: see NOTORIETY- FOR- PROFIT LEGISLATION.

SUBROGATION: the substitution of a creditor who assumes responsibility for payment and the right to collect it from a third party; for example, state crime victim compensation programs subrogate victims' rights to collect from offenders and other third parties responsible for victims' expenses.

UNJUST ENRICHMENT: victim compensation that benefits the offender; most state crime victim compensation programs have statutes prohibiting this.

VICTIMS' MOVEMENT: a combination of activities that have as their professed aim an increase in victims' rights; experts suggest that many of these activities only reduce the rights of offenders, and therefore benefit the criminal justice system, but not victims.

VICTIMS' RIGHTS: legislation having as its professed aim an increase in the ways in which victims' needs are addressed by the criminal justice and social welfare systems. Many so-called victims' rights affect few victims, such as those whose cases go to trial, and may induce people to claim to be victims who are not.

Bibliography

AFL-CIO Executive Council on Prison Labor Programs. *Position Statement on Prison Labor Programs.* Washington, D. C.: AFL-CIO, 1991.

Aharoni, Y. *The No-Risk Society.* Chatham, N.J.: Chatham House Publishers, 1981.

Alabama Crime Victims Compensation Commission. *Annual Report 1990-1991.* Montgomery, Ala.: Alabama Crime Victims Compensation Commission, 1991.

Antilla, I. "From Crime Policy to Victim Policy?" In *From Crime Policy to Victim Policy: Reorienting the Justice System,* ed. E. Fattah. New York: St. Martin's Press, 1986, 237-45.

Arkansas Workers' Compensation Commission. *Arkansas Workers' Compensation Commission Biennial Report, 1990-1992.* Little Rock, Ark: Arkansas Workers' Compensation Commission, 1993.

"Auction of Land Draws Few Bids from Hungary." *New York Times,* September 6, 1992, 19.

"Auction to Sell Dahmer Items Is Now Unlikely." *New York Times,* May 29, 1996.

Barbieri, M. "Civil Suits for Sexual Assault Victims: The Downside." *Journal of Interpersonal Violence* 4, no. 1, (March 1989): 110-113.

Barnett, R., and J. Hagel. "Assessing the Criminal." In *Assessing The Criminal: Restitution, Retribution and the Criminal Process,* ed. R. Barnett and J. Hagel. Cambridge, Mass.: Ballinger, 1977, 1-31.

Bastian, L. "Hispanic Victims." *Bureau of Justice Statistics Special Report.* Washington, D.C.: U.S. Department of Justice, January 1990.

Bendick, M. "Failure to Enroll in Public Assistance Programs." *Social Work,* July 1980, 268-80.

Bendick, M., and M. Cantu. "The Literacy of Welfare Clients." *Social Service Review* 52, March 1978, 56-68.

Benjamin, D., and R. Miller. *Undoing Drugs.* New York: Basic Books, 1991.

Besharov, D., and S. Besharov. "Teaching About Liability." *Social Work,* November-December 1987, 517-21.

"Betting Odds: News or Not?" *American Journalism Review,* July 1995.

Biderman, A., and Lynch, J. *Understanding Crime Incidence Statistics.* New York: Springer-Verlag, 1991.

Binder, D. "Jews of Nazi Era Get Claims Details." *New York Times,* December 22, 1992.

Box-Grainger, J. "Sentencing Rapists." In *Confronting Crime*, ed. R. Matthews and J. Young. London: Sage Publications, 1986, 31-52.

Bradshaw, J. "The Concept of Social Need." In *Planning For Social Welfare: Issues, Tasks, and Models*, ed. N. Gilbert and H. Specht. Englewood Cliffs, N.J.: Prentice Hall, 1977.

Brants, C., and E. Koh. "Penal Sanctions as a Feminist Strategy: Contradiction in Terms." *International Journal of The Sociology of Law*, 14, 1986, 269-86.

Bryant, C. "Evaluating Contributory Conduct." *National Association of Crime Victim Compensation Boards Report*, November/December 1990, 7-15.

Carey, M. "It's Time to Amend Our Community Correction Acts to Restorative Justice Acts." Unpublished, 1995.

Carlson, K. "Estimating the Total Number of Persons Eligible for Crime Victim Compensation." In *Compensating Crime Victims*, ed. D. Parent, B. Auerbach, and K. Carlson. Washington, D.C.: U. S. Department of Justice, January 1992.

Carrington, F., and J. Rapp. *Victims' Rights: Law and Litigation*. New York: Matthew Bender, 1989.

Carrow, D. *Crime Victim Compensation: Program Models*. Washington, D.C.: U. S. Department of Justice, 1980.

Chambers, D., K. Wedel, and M. Rodwell. *Evaluating Social Programs*. Boston, MA: Allyn and Bacon, 1992.

Chappell, D. "Providing for the Victims of Crime: Political Placebos or Progressive Programs?" *Adelaide Law Review*, 4, 294, 1972.

Cleary, C. "Litigating Incest Torts." *National Insurance Law Review* 3, 2, 1989, 155-178.

"COBRA." *Tax Management Compensation Planning Journal*, July 7, 1995, 180-181.

"Complying with VOCA's New Terrorism Requirement." Alexandria, Va.: *Crime Victim Compensation Quarterly*, Spring 1996.

Crenshaw, A. "Covered Against Fire, Theft and Cheaters." *Washington Post Weekly*, June 21-7, 1993.

Currie, E. *Confronting Crime*. New York: Pantheon, 1985.

Cutler, W. "The Cutting Edge—How Americans Become Uninsured." *Washington Post*, 5, July 5, 1994.

Davis, R., and M. Henley. "Victim Service Programs." In *Victims of Crime: Problems, Policies and Programs,* ed. Lurigio, A., W. Skogan, and R. Davis. Beverly Hills, Calif.: Sage Publications, 1990, 157-71.

DeFrancis, C. et al. *Civil Jury Cases and Verdicts in Large Counties*. Washington, D.C.: U.S. Department of Justice, July 1995.

Delaware State Law. Chapter 90, Secs. 9001- 9018. *Compensation For Innocent Victims of Crime.*

DiMascio, W. *Seeking Justice*. New York: The Edna McConnell Clark Foundation, 1995.

Donnerstein, E., D. Linz, and S. Penrod . *The Question of Pornography: Research Findings and Policy Implications.* New York: Free Press, 1987.

Dooley, M. "Restorative Justice in Vermont: A Work in Progress." In *Topics in Community Corrections 1995*. Washington, D.C.: U.S. Department of Justice, 1995.

Dulberg, B. *Social and Psychological Factors Inhibiting Use of Crime Victims Compensation Board.* Unpublished Master's Thesis, John Jay College of Criminal Justice of the City University of New York, February 1978.

Eddy, D. "Health Care Reform: Cure for Compensation Budgets?" *Crime Victims Compensation Quarterly*, 3, 1992, 7-11.

Edelwich, J. *Burn-Out*. New York: Human Sciences Press, 1980.

Eglash, A. "Beyond Restitution—Creative Restitution." In *Restitution in Criminal Justice* ed. J. Hudson and B. Galaway. Lexington, Mass.: Lexington Books, 1977, 91-99.

Elden, G. " 'Forty Acres and a Mule' with Interest: The Constitutionality of Black Capitalism, Benign School Quotas, and Other Statutory Racial Classifications." *Journal of Urban Law*, 47, no. 3, 1970, 591-652.

Elias, R. *Victims Still*. Newbury Park, Calif.: Sage Publications, 1993.

―――. "Community Control, Criminal Justice and Victim Services." In *Toward a Critical Victimology* ed. E. Fattah. London: Macmillan, 1992, 372-400

―――. *Victims of the System: Crime Victims and Compensation in American Politics and Criminal Justice*. New Brunswick, N. J.: Transaction Books, 1983.

Epstein, R. "Crime and Tort: Old Wine in Old Bottles." In *Assessing the Criminal: Restitution, Retribution and the Legal Process*, ed. R. Barnett and J. Hagel. Cambridge, Mass.: Ballinger, 1977, 231-57.

Federal Emergency Management Agency. *Federal Crime Insurance Program: Commercial and Residential - Information*. Rockville, Md: Federal Emergency Management Agency, September 1989, 1-11.

Finkelhor, D. and Associates. *A Sourcebook on Child Sexual Assault*. Beverly Hills, Calif.: Sage Publications, 1986.

Franklin, H. *Prison Literature in America*. New York: Oxford University Press, 1989.

Fry, M. "Justice for Victims." *Journal of Public Law*, 8, 1959, 191-194.

Galaway, B., and J. Hudson, eds. *Perspectives on Crime Victims*. St. Louis, Mo: C. V. Mosby Co., 1981.

Galper, J. *The Politics of Social Services*. Englewood Cliffs, N.J.: Prentice-Hall, 1975.

Garofalo, R. "Enforced Reparation as a Substitute for Imprisonment." In *Considering the Victim: Readings in Restitution and Victim Compensation*, ed. J. Hudson and B. Galaway. Springfield, Ill.: Charles C. Thomas, Publisher, 1975, 43-53.

Gates, B. *Social Program Administration*. Englewood Cliffs, N.J.: Prentice-Hall, 1980.

Geis, G. "State Compensation to Victims of Violent Crime." President's Commission on Law Enforcement and Administration of Justice. *Task Force Report: Crime and its Impact—An Assessment*. Washington, D.C.: U.S. Department of Justice, 1967.

Gilbert, N. *Capitalism And The Welfare State: Dilemmas of Social Benevolence*. New Haven, Conn.: Yale University Press, 1983.

Gilbert, N., H. Specht, and P. Terrell. *Dimensions of Social Welfare Policy*, Third Edition. Englewood Cliffs, N.J.: Prentice-Hall, 1993.

Goffman, E. *Stigma: Notes on The Management of Spoiled Identity*. Englewood Cliffs, N.J.: Prentice-Hall, 1963.

Goldberg, C. "Inmate Upsets Seizure Policy on Drugs." *New York Times*, April 7, 1996.

Goldberg, G. *Government Money for Everyday People*. New York: Ginn Press for Adelphi University, 1991.

Goldstein, M. "When Criminal Lawyers Go Hollywood." *Newsday*, September 4, 1992, 6, 39.

Goldstein, N. "Reparation by the Offender to the Victim as a Method of Rehabilitation for Both." In *Victimology— A New Focus*, ed. I. Drapkin and E. Viano. Lexington, Mass: Lexington Books, 1974, 193-206.

Grady, M. "Insurance Coverage for Sexually Molested Minors." *Defense Council Journal*, 56, no. 2, April 1989, 170-8.

Guarino, R., and R. Trubo. *The Great American Insurance Hoax*. Los Angeles, Calif.: Nash Publishing, 1974.

Gummer, B. *The Politics of Social Administration: Managing Organizational Politics in Social Agencies*. Englewood Cliffs, N.J.: Prentice-Hall, 1990.

Harland, A. "Theoretical and Programmatic Concerns in Restitution: An Integration." In *Offender Restitution in Theory and Action*, ed. B. Galaway and J. Hudson. Lexington, Mass.: Lexington Books, 1978, 193-202.

Harris, L. *Victims of Crime: A Research Report of Experiencing Victimization*. New York: Garland Publishing, 1984.

Hasenfeld, Y. *Human Service Organizations*. Englewood Cliffs, N.J.: Prentice-Hall, 1983.

Hawaii Department of Labor and Industrial Relations. *Hawaii Workers' Compensation Databook 1992*. Honolulu, Haw.: Department of Labor and Industrial Relations, 1993.

Hay, P. *The Book of Legal Anecdotes*. New York: Facts on File, 1989.

Hazelip, D. *Notoriety for Profit Legislation*. Unpublished Master's Thesis, California State University at Sacramento, 1987.

Heilbroner, D. "The Law Goes on a Treasure Hunt." *New York Times Magazine*, December 11, 1994, 70-3.

Heins, M. "Punishing Sexual Crimes: A New and Dangerous Approach." *Civil Liberties*, Spring 1992.

Henderson, L. "The Wrongs of Victims' Rights." *Stanford Law Review* 37, 1985, 937-1021.

Hernandez, R. "State Is Ruled Accountable Over Child Abuse Phone Line." *New York Times*, March 2, 1996.

Herrnstein, R., and C. Murray. *The Bell Curve*. New York: The Free Press, 1994.

Hevesi, D. "U. S. High Court Will Decide if 'Son of Sam' Law is Legal." *New York Times*, February 20, 1991, B8.

"High Court Upsets Seizing Profits on Convicts' Books." *New York Times*, December 11, 1991, A1.

Hindelang, M., and M. Gottfredson. "The Victim's Decision Not to Invoke the Criminal Justice Process." In *Criminal Justice And The Victim*, ed. W. McDonald. Beverly Hills, Calif: Sage Publications, 1986, 57-78.

Hockenberry, J. *Moving Violations*. New York: Hyperion, 1995.

Hoffman, J. "Subway Rape Victim Tries to Prove Agency Was at Fault." *New York Times*, August 31, 1995.

Huber, P., and R. Litan, eds. *The Liability Maze*. Washington, D.C.: The Brookings Institution, 1991.

Iowa Department of Justice. Chapter 9, Division II: *Crime Victim Reparation Administrative Rules*. Iowa Department of Justice, undated.

Jacob, B. "The Concept of Restitution: An Historical Overview." In *Restitution in Criminal Justice*, ed. J. Hudson and B. Galaway. Lexington, Mass.: Lexington Books, 1977, 45-62.

Jencks. C. *Rethinking Social Policy*. Cambridge, Mass.: Harvard University Press, 1992.

Jones, E. "The Costs of Victim Compensation." In *The Costs of Crime*, ed. C. Gray. Beverly Hills, Calif.: Sage Publications, 1979, 121-48.

"Jury Awards $1M to Couple Exposed by Hotel's Mirror." *Newsday*, June 27, 1992, 9.

"Justices Uphold Civil Forfeiture as Anti-Drug Tool." *New York Times*, June 25, 1996.

Kahn, A. "Perspectives on Access to Social Service." *Social Work*, 15, no.2, March 1970.

Kansas Crime Victims Compensation Board. *Policy Guidelines*. Kansas Crime Victims Compensation Board, undated.

Karmen, A. "The Controversy over Shared Responsibility." In *To Be a Victim*, ed. D. Sank and D. Kaplan. New York: Plenum Press, 1991, 395-408.

———. *Crime Victims*, Second Edition. Monterey, Calif.: Brooks/Cole, 1990.

Kelly, B. *Adventures in Porkland*. New York: Villard Books, 1992.

Kidd, R., and E. Chayet. "Why Do Victims Fail to Report? The Psychology of Criminal Victimization." *Journal of Social Issues*, 1, 1984, 39-50.

Kluger, R. "A Peace Plan for Cigarette Wars." *New York Times Magazine*, April 7, 1996.

Knudten, R. et al. "The Victim in the Administration of Criminal Justice: Problems and Perceptions." In *Criminal Justice And The Victim*, ed. W. McDonald. Beverly Hills, Calif.: Sage Publications, 1976, 115-146.

Kremen, E. *Battered Women in Counseling And Shelter Programs: A Descriptive and Follow-up Study*. Ann Arbor, Mich.: University Microfilms International, 1984.

Kuh, R. *Testimony Before The New York Governor's Committee on The Compensation of Victims of Violent Crime*. January 3, 1966.

Kuntzman, G. "Auction Houses Refuse Dahmer's 'Murderabilia'." *New York Post*, May 5, 1996.

Kuttner, R. "Killing the Lawyers." *Washington Post Weekly*, April 8-14, 1996.

Levinson, R. *Information And Referral Networks: Doorways to Human Services*. New York: Springer Publishing, 1988.

Lewin, T. "An Unpaid Debt," sidebar to a review of *Dark Obsession: a True Story of Incest and Justice. New York Times Book Review*, February 25, 1990.

Lifton, R. "The Broken Connection." *Evaluation and Change*, Special Issue, 1980, 55-70.

Lindblom, C. *The Policy-Making Process*. Englewood Cliffs, N.J.: Prentice-Hall, 1980.

London, R. "Sending a $12.5 Million Message to a Hate Group." *New York Times*, October 26, 1990.

McCombs, P. "The Goldman Family's Trial of Tears." *Newsday*, November 7, 1995.

McElroy, W. "The New Mythology of Rape." *Liberty*, September 1994.

McGillis, D. *Crime Victim Restitution: An Analysis of Approaches*. Washington, D.C.: U.S. Department of Justice, December 1986.

Maguire, K., and A. Pastore. *Sourcebook of Criminal Justice Statistics 1994*. Albany, N.Y.: Hindelang Criminal Justice Research Center, 1994.

Maslach, C. "Job Burnout: How People Cope." *Public Welfare*, Spring 1978, 56-8.

Matthews, J. "The Quiet Move Toward Benefits for Gay Couples." *Washington Post Weekly*, October 11-17, 1993, 22.

Media Monitor. " 'Media Crime Wave' Continues—Crime News Quadrupled in Four Years." Washington, D.C.: Center for Media and Public Affairs, January/February 1996.

Mehr, R., and E. Cammack. *Principles of Insurance*. Homewood, Ill.: Richard D. Irwin, Inc., 1980.

Miller, T., M. Cohen, and B. Wiersema. *Victim Costs and Consequences: A New Look.* Washington, D.C.: U.S. Department of Justice, February 1996.

Mokhiber, R. *Corporate Crime and Violence*. San Francisco: Sierra Club Books, 1988.

Mueller, G., and H. Cooper. "Society and the Victim: Alternative Responses." In *Victimology: A New Focus*, ed. I. Drapkin and E. Viano. Lexington, Mass.: Lexington Books, 1975, 85-101.

Nader, L., and E. Combs-Schilling. "Restitution in Cross-Cultural Perspective." In *Restitution in Criminal Justice*, ed. J. Hudson and B. Galaway. Lexington, Mass.: D. C. Heath, 1977.

Nassau County Community Services Agency. *Community Services: Who, What, When, Where, Why & How*. Mineola, N. Y.: NCCSA, 1989.

National Association of Crime Victim Compensation Boards. *The Compensation Academy*. Washington, D.C.: NACVCB, November 1994a

———. "Maximums and Expense Limits." *Crime Victim Compensation Quarterly*, no. 2, 1994b.

————. *Crime Victim Compensation Program Directory 1993.* Washington, D.C.: NACVCB, 1993.

————. "Victim Issues in Supreme Court." *Crime Victim Compensation Quarterly.* Washington, D.C.: NACVCB Boards, no. 1, 1991.

National Association of Social Workers Delegates Assembly. *Code of Ethics of The National Association of Social Workers.* Washington, D.C.: National Association of Social Workers, 1979.

Nelson A. Rockefeller Institute of Government. *1987-88 New York State Statistical Yearbook,* 14th ed. Albany, N.Y.: Nelson A. Rockefeller Institute of Government, 1989.

New Jersey State Law. Chapter 4B, Secs. 1-38. *Criminal Injuries Compensation Act of 1971.*

New Jersey Violent Crimes Compensation Board. *Annual Report, July 1, 1989 - June 30, 1990.* Trenton, N.J.: New Jersey Violent Crimes Compensation Board, 1990.

New Mexico Crime Victims Reparation Commission. *Regulations.* New Mexico Crime Victims Reparation Commission, 1991.

New York State Clients' Security Fund. *Annual Report 1986.* New York: Clients' Security Fund, 1987.

New York State Crime Victims Board. *Compensation Procedure Manual.* New York: New York State Crime Victims Board, 1990.

New York State Division of Criminal Justice Services and New York State Crime Victims Board. *Restitution in New York State: Recommendations for Improvement.* New York: New York State Division of Criminal Justice Services and New York State Crime Victims Board, June 1988.

New York State Legislative Commission on Expenditure Review. *Crime Victims Board Programs.* New York: The Legislature of the State of New York, 1975.

Nishimura, G. *Membership Solicitation Letter.* Washington, D.C.: HALT (Help Abolish Legal Tyranny), 1990.

Office for Victims of Crime. *Civil Remedies for Crime Victims.* Washington, D.C.: U. S. Department of Justice, December 1993.

————. *Victims of Crime Act Victim Compensation Grant Program.* U.S. Department of Justice, undated.

O'Neill, T. "The Good, the Bad and the Burger Court." *Journal of Criminal Law And Criminology* 75, 1984, 363-87.

Onishi, N. "Youth Drops Accusation About Police." *New York Times,* August 7, 1995.

Parent, D., B. Auerbach, and K. Carlson. *Compensating Crime Victims.* Washington, D.C.: U. S. Department of Justice, January 1992.

Parenti, C. "Inside Jobs." *New Statesman and Society,* November 3, 1995, 20.

Pennsylvania Crime Victims' Compensation Board. *Loss of Earnings Eligibility Policy.* Pennsylvania Crime Victims' Compensation Board, April 1992.

Pinkerton, J. *What Comes Next?* New York: Hyperion, 1995.

Piven, F., and R. Cloward. *Regulating The Poor: The Functions of Public Welfare.* New York: Vintage Books, 1993.

Purdy, M. "Workplace Murders Provoke Lawsuits and Better Security." *New York Times,* February 14, 1994.

Reiman, J. *The Rich Get Richer and the Poor Get Prison,* 2nd ed. New York: John Wiley and Sons, 1984.

"Restitution Payments Readied for Oldest WWII Internees." *Los Angeles Times,* August 2, 1990, 24.

Roth, J. "Some Contingencies of the Moral Evaluation and Control of Clientele: The Case of the Hospital Emergency Service." In *Human Service Organizations,* ed. Y. Hasenfeld and R. English. Ann Arbor, Mich.: University of Michigan Press, 1974, 499-516.

Rudovsky, D. "Crime, Law Enforcement and Constitutional Rights." In *A Less Than Perfect Union* ed. J. Lobel. New York: Monthly Review Press, 1988, 361-76.

Samuelson, R. *The Good Life And Its Discontents.* New York: Random House, 1995.

Schafer, S. *Victimology: the Victim and His Criminal.* Reston, Virg.: Prentice-Hall, 1977

————. *Compensation And Restitution to Victims of Crime.* Montclair, N.J.: Patterson Smith, 1970.

Schechter, S. *Women And Male Violence.* Boston, Mass.: South End Press, 1984.

Separovic, Z. *Victimology.* Zagreb, Yugoslavia: Pravni Fakultet, 1985.

Shapland, J. "Victims and the Criminal Justice System." In *From Crime Policy to Victim Policy,* ed. E. Fattah. New York: St. Martin's Press, 1986, 210-7.

Siemaszko, C. "Dahmer Gear Sale to Aid Victims' Kin." *New York Daily News,* April 25, 1996.

Singer, J., M. Neale, and G. Schwartz. "The Nuts and Bolts of Assessing Occupational Stress: A Collaborative Effort with Labor." In *Stress Management in Work Settings,* ed. L. Murphey and T. Schoenborn. Cincinnati, Ohio: U.S. Department of Health and Human Services, National Institute for Occupational Safety and Health, May 1987, 3-29.

Skocpol, T. *Protecting Soldiers And Mothers.* Cambridge, Mass.: Harvard University Press, 1992.

Smith, G., and P. Schwartzman. "Suing for Lives Lost to Abuse." *New York Daily News,* October 23, 1995.

Smith, S. and S. Freinkel. *Adjusting The Balance: Federal Policy and Victim Services.* New York: Greenwood Press, 1988.

Sobieski, R. "Legislative News." *MADDVOCATE* 4, no.2, Winter 1991, 5-7.

Spence, G. *With Justice For None.* New York: Times Books, 1989.

Stark, J., and H. Goldstein. *The Rights of Crime Victims.* New York: Bantam Books for the American Civil Liberties Union, 1985.

Sullivan, J. "Car Insurance Covers Shooting, Court Says." *New York Times,* December 20, 1994, B5.

Sunny von Bulow Victim Advocacy Center with the Attorney's Victim Assistance Project of the American Bar Association Criminal Justice Section. *The Attorneys' Victim Assistance Manual.* Fort Worth, Tex.: Sunny von Bulow National Victim Advocacy Center, December 1987.

Tavris, C. "Beware the Incest-Survivor Machine." *New York Times Book Review,* January 3, 1993, 1, 16-7.

Tayler, L. "Long Island a Law Theft Hotspot." *Newsday,* March 10, 1992, 22.

United States Department of Health and Human Services. *Directory of Facilities Obligated to Provide Hill-Burton Uncompensated Services by State and City.* Washington, D.C.: U. S. Department of Health and Human Services, January 1994.

United States Department of Justice. *Office of Justice Programs Application Kit: Stop Violence Against Women.* Washington, D.C.: U.S. Department of Justice, 1995a.

————. *Work in American Prisons: Joint Ventures with the Private Sector.* Washington, D.C.: U.S. Department of Justice, November 1995b.

————. *Civil Legal Remedies For Crime Victims.* Washington, D.C.: U.S. Department of Justice, December 1993.

———.   *Restitution and Juvenile Recidivists.* Washington, D.C.: U.S. Department of Justice, September 1992.

———.   *Office For Victims of Crime Report to Congress.* Washington, D.C.: U.S. Department of Justice, April 1990.

———.   *Office For Victims of Crime Report to Congress.* Washington, D.C.: U.S. Department of Justice, March 1988a.

———.   *Report to the Nation on Crime and Justice.* Washington, D.C.: U.S. Department of Justice, March 1988b.

———.   *Indexed Legislative History of the Victims of Crime Act of 1984.* Washington. D.C.: U.S. Department of Justice, 1984a.

———.   *Victim/Witness Legislation: An Overview.* Washington, D.C.: U.S. Department of Justice, July 1984b.

———.   *President's Task Force on Victims of Crime: Final Report.* Washington, D.C.: U.S. Department of Justice, 1982.

———.   *Victims of Crime Act Crime Victims Fund.* Washington, D.C.: U.S. Department of Justice, undated.

United States Department of the Treasury. *1995 1040 Instructions.* Washington, D.C.: U.S. Government Printing Office, 1995.

United States General Accounting Office Community and Economic Development Division. *Federal Crime Insurance Program—An Overview.* Washington, D.C.: U.S. General Accounting Office, 1981.

Valente, J. "They Steal from the Devastated." *Parade*, June 4, 1995.

VanGelder, L. "Victim's Wife Files Lawsuit in NBC Killing." *New York Times*, September 21, 1994.

Verhovek, S. "Lawmakers in Agreement on 'Son of Sam' Measure." *New York Times*, July 3, 1992, B4.

"Vermont Authorizes Restitution to Compensation." *Crime Victims Compensation Quarterly,* 1994, 5.

Victims' Assistance Legal Organization, Inc. *Restitution: Policies And Procedures For a Coordinated Team Model.* (Draft) McLean, Virg.: VALOR, March 1996.

"Victims' Rights Amendments Pass in 5 States." *New York Times*, November 8, 1992, 29.

Villmoare, E., and V. Neto. *Victim Appearances at Sentencing under California's Victims' Bill of Rights.* Washington, D.C.: U.S. Department of Justice, August 1987.

Virginia Division of Crime Victims Compensation. Chapter 21.1, Secs. 19.2-368-19.2-368.18. *Compensating Victims of Crime.* Virginia Division of Crime Victims Compensation, undated.

Whitaker, C. "Black Victims." *Bureau of Justice Statistics Special Report,* April 1990.

Widom, C. *The Cycle of Violence.* Washington, D.C.: U.S. Department of Justice, September 1992.

Wilson, J. *Thinking About Crime.* New York: Basic Books, 1975.

Wilson, W. *The Truly Disadvantaged.* Chicago: University of Chicago Press, 1987.

Wolfgang, M. "Victim Compensation in Crimes of Personal Violence." *Minnesota Law Review* 50, 1965.

Woolhandler, S., and D. Himmelstein. "The Deteriorating Efficiency of the U. S. Health Care System." *The New England Journal of Medicine* 324, no. 18, May 2, 1991, 1253-1257.

Ziegenhagen, E. *Victims of Violent Crimes in New York City: An Exploratory Study of Perceived Needs.* Unpublished report to the Crime Victim's Consultation Project, New York, 1974.

Index

About the Author

SUSAN KISS SARNOFF has worked in the field of crime victim advocacy for the past two decades. She is a founder and former director of the Adelphi Resource Center for Crime Victim Advocates at Adelphi University.